A 6-WEEK BIBLE STUDY EXPERIENCE

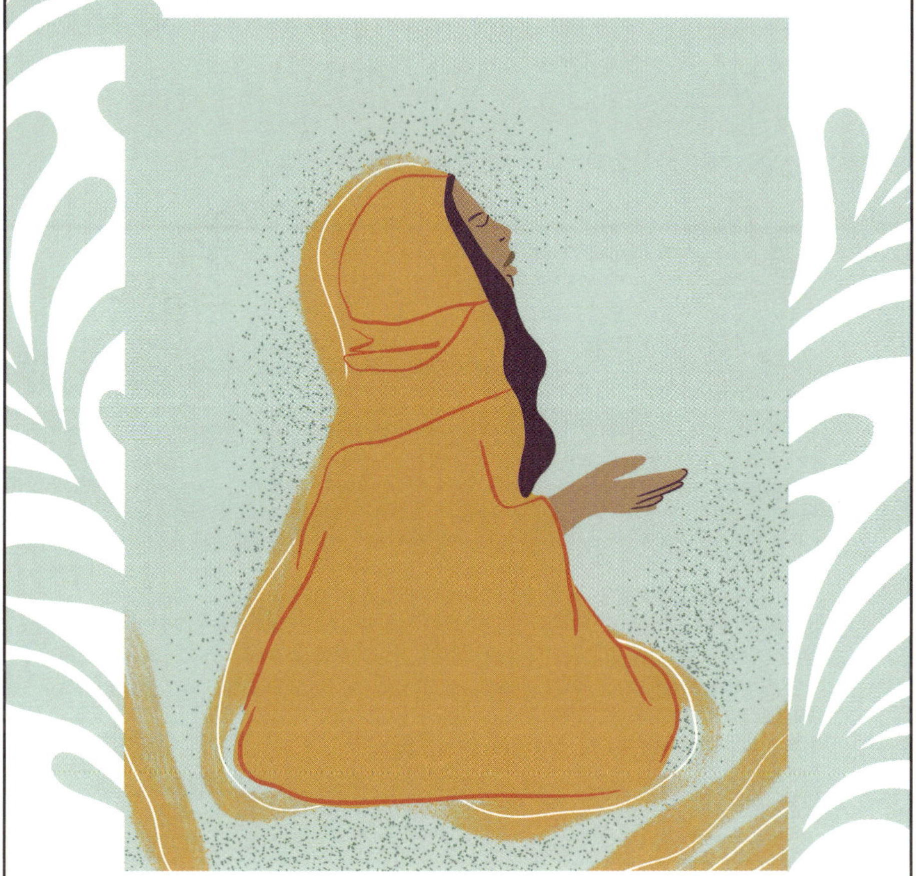

REDEEMER

God's Lovingkindness in the Book of Ruth

DORINA LAZO GILMORE-YOUNG

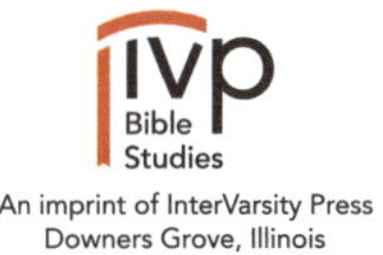

ivp Bible Studies
An imprint of InterVarsity Press
Downers Grove, Illinois

InterVarsity Press
P.O. Box 1400 | Downers Grove, IL 60515-1426
ivpress.com | email@ivpress.com

InterVarsity Press® is the publishing division of InterVarsity Christian Fellowship/USA®. For more information, visit intervarsity.org.

Published in association with the Books & Such Literary Management, https://www.booksandsuch.com.

While any stories in this book are true, some names and identifying information may have been changed to protect the privacy of individuals.

Art by Octavia Mingerink, www.prettyininkpress.com. Used by permission.

The publisher cannot verify the accuracy or functionality of website URLs used in this book beyond the date of publication.

Cover design: David Fassett
Interior design: Jeanna Wiggins
Cover image: Octavia Mingerink

ISBN 978-1-5140-0835-5 (print) | ISBN 978-1-5140-0836-2 (digital)

Printed in the United States of America ♾

Library of Congress Cataloging-in-Publication Data

Names: Gilmore-Young, Dorina Lazo, author.
Title: Redeemer : God's lovingkindness in the book of ruth-a 6-week Bible study experience / Dorina Lazo Gilmore-Young.
Description: Downers Grove, IL : InterVarsity Press, [2025] | Series: IVP Bible studies | Includes bibliographical references.
Identifiers: LCCN 2024031180 (print) | LCCN 2024031181 (ebook) | ISBN 9781514008355 (print) | ISBN 9781514008362 (digital)
Subjects: LCSH: Bible. Ruth–Commentaries. | Bible–Study and teaching
Classification: LCC BS1315.3 .G56 2025 (print) | LCC BS1315.3 (ebook) | DDC 222/.3507–dc23/eng/20241002
LC record available at https://lccn.loc.gov/2024031180
LC ebook record available at https://lccn.loc.gov/2024031181

30 29 28 27 26 25 | 8 7 6 5 4 3 2 1

Contents

Introduction

MY FASCINATION WITH THE BOOK OF RUTH began when I was learning to make my faith my own. Only two books in the Bible are named after women—Ruth and Esther—and I had a deep desire to learn about both of these "herstories." I wanted to learn more about these books that centered women in the story and didn't merely make them supporting characters.

As a young woman, I admired Ruth for her loyalty, her strong work ethic, and her kindness toward her mother-in-law. Ruth showed us what these character qualities looked like in real life.

The book of Ruth was a beautiful, fairy-tale story to me. I revered it as such. Of course, I had no idea that a few decades later I would find myself relating to Ruth in a much more powerful and personal way than I'd ever imagined.

The book of Ruth became real to me when I was widowed at thirty-seven. My husband was diagnosed with stage four melanoma cancer in May and soared to heaven that September, leaving me with three young daughters and a shattered heart. Just a few months after his funeral, I attended a Bible study at my church where they were studying the book of Ruth. God helped me find him anew through the pages of this book. Suddenly, Ruth was no longer a fairy tale to me. This was a living, breathing story of God's heart for vulnerable women like Ruth and like me.

My heart was captivated in the first chapter when we were introduced to three widows—one older and two younger. I felt the gravity of their situation in a new way. I wept with these women. Their sorrow was my sorrow. I understood the bond between them in a much greater way because of what I had lost and endured. I learned to navigate grief alongside these women.

Like Ruth and her mother-in-law Naomi, I discovered that the grief journey is lonely and strange and unpredictable. Frequently, grief either strengthens or challenges our faith in God because it forces us to grapple with suffering. When we grieve, we wonder about pain, death, and the afterlife. This is something we will witness from both Ruth and Naomi.

Ruth is not simply a love story with a predictable Hallmark plot and a kiss to seal the deal at the end. Ruth is a book about God's providence in the midst of tragedy. Ruth is about dealing with disappointment, traversing trials, wrestling with grief, and deepening faith. Ruth is about a courageous woman and a kind man who each illustrate for us the heart and character of God. And perhaps too often overlooked, Ruth is a story about God's heart for the marginalized.

The book of Ruth is not *only* for women, but it's a book that is important for women. Why? Because it reminds us that God is *for* women and that God shows particular concern for vulnerable women. Regardless of your circumstances and experience, you need to know that *you* matter to God.

Ruth is also part of history—God's story—the story of the Son of God who was sent to earth to be the ultimate Redeemer for us all. It's about a foreigner, an immigrant, a widow, a daughter, who is invited to return to Naomi's home, to Bethlehem, where God shows her unexpected lovingkindness, grace, mercy, and abundant provision. Ruth's story reminds us that God has offered redemption—not just for the Israelites but for all the nations and for all of us.

God showed me his abundant kindness on the gritty trail of my life. Through wild "just-so-happened" circumstances, God brought me through by his goodness and grace, and I'm living out the details of that next chapter today. Of course, all our stories are different, and our journeys are unique. So Ruth's story isn't an instruction book telling us how to navigate challenges and hardships. Instead, in our study of this book we'll discover that our good and great God sees us, knows us, and is in the business of redeeming the pain and brokenness in our lives. Ruth's story illustrates for us God's remarkable, redemptive love.

I'm excited to be able to explore that love with you during the next six weeks. May our time together grow and deepen our understanding of our Lord as we explore his care for the vulnerable and his wondrous love for us.

How to Use This Study

REDEEMER IS DESIGNED TO BE USED by individuals or small groups. I recommend you watch the teaching video as a group and then go into discussion and prayer together each week. For groups following this study, I recommend allowing at least forty-five minutes for discussion (or more for larger groups). Following your weekly time as a group, which serves as an introduction, there are five days of study and reflection to explore on your own. Each week of this study will focus on a different part of the book of Ruth.

As you're working through this study, I encourage you to go at your own pace. Let's be curious and open our hearts to new insights. The first four days will provide verse-by-verse reading, context, and teaching. Day five will be more of a reflective day, incorporating visual art, Scripture for you to meditate on, and space for prayer.

Friend, I'm eager to study this book with you. Grab your backpack, your Bible, and a water bottle. It's a dusty road, but this path leads us straight to Bethlehem and God's miraculous provision.

WEEK ONE

Following the Path to Bethlehem

RUTH 1

GROUP SESSION: THE TURNING POINT

Today we are going to talk about turning points in our lives. A turning point is when the action, the energy, or perhaps the circumstances change. The book of Ruth drops us right into a major turning point in the lives of our main characters.

WATCH

Take some time now to **WATCH** the video that accompanies the week one study.

READ

READ Ruth 1:1-22.

DISCUSS

1. What are some of the questions you have brought with you to this study of the book of Ruth?

2. In today's video, you heard about a turning point in my life and in Ruth's life. Is there a time that felt like a turning point in your life? If so, share with the group something about that experience.

3. One of the themes that emerges in the book of the Ruth is God's heart for the vulnerable. READ the following passages aloud and notice what they tell us about God and his heart of mercy. Take a few minutes to list some of those characteristics of God in the space below.

Deuteronomy 10:18-19

Psalm 146:5-9

James 1:27

4. Looking at that list, name something that either surprises you about God, or something that you struggle to accept about him.

5. Who are the vulnerable women in your community?

6. What conditions led to their vulnerability?

7. What is one small thing you can do to honor these women today? Maybe it's looking someone in the eyes, stopping for a conversation, or taking time to learn more about these women in your community. Brainstorm some ideas together.

8. In the video, I shared about how Ruth starts out as helpless and moves toward hopeful. Are you or someone close to you facing anything in life that feels helpless? If you are comfortable, share this with others.

PRAY

As you close your time, I've included a few suggestions to guide you in prayer together:

- Thank God for who he is, naming those characteristics we read in Scripture.
- Ask God to meet you and others in circumstances that feel helpless.
- Ask God to comfort and provide for the women in your community who might be feeling helpless in different ways.
- Ask for courage and wisdom to honor the vulnerable women in your community.

If you prefer, write out a prayer in the margins or in a journal.

MEMORY VERSE

WEEK ONE

Ruth replied, "Don't urge me to leave you or to turn back from you. Where you go I will go, and where you stay I will stay. Your people will be my people and your God my God. Where you die I will die, and there I will be buried. May the Lord deal with me, be it ever so severely, if even death separates you and me."

Ruth 1:16-17

DAY ONE • What's in a Name?

LOOK back over Ruth 1. How might you describe this chapter in a word or a feeling? What title would you give this chapter?

My first job out of college was as a newspaper reporter at *The Fresno Bee* in Central California. That led to a teaching opportunity where I walked students through the principles of investigative journalism. They learned that a top-notch article nails six questions: Who? What? When? Where? Why? and How?

Because the book of Ruth is exquisitely written, we want to start this journey with the posture of an investigative journalist. Answering these questions will enhance our understanding of the book of Ruth, the context in which these events take place, and the significance of Ruth herself in the greater biblical narrative.

REVIEW Ruth 1:1-5.

List the principal figures in this chapter and how they are related or connected.

In his timeless play *Romeo and Juliet*, Shakespeare penned Juliet's famous protest: "What's in a name? That which we call a rose by any other name would smell as sweet." Juliet's words try to say that names are not important. She loves Romeo whether he is a Montague or not. Her love for him is deep and pure. She doesn't care about his name or his family affiliation. Of course, through the play, we learn that it's not that simple. Names do matter in surprisingly deep ways. Names often carry our stories, our family legacy, our connection to our cultural heritage, and more.

In the book of Ruth and in the Bible in general, the meaning of names is significant. Names also gave an indication of who the person might become. *Naomi* means "my joy" and "pleasant" in Hebrew, while *Ruth* means "friendship." As we follow along in this story, we will see why both names are significant. *Elimelek* means "my God is King," while his sons are named *Mahlon*, meaning "sick and dying," and *Kilion*, meaning "puny and tiny." Sometimes biblical names are unfortunate and ironic, but they're worth paying attention to because they add to our understanding of the context.

REVIEW Ruth 1:19-21.

What does Naomi tell her people to call her and what does this indicate about the condition of her heart when she arrives in Bethlehem?

It's curious to me that even though Naomi (or, now, Mara) experiences so much hardship, she continues to call God "the Almighty," showing she still trusts him. Perhaps she was able to hold on to such faith because she recalled another woman who endured much hardship and calamity in her life: Hagar. In fact, Hagar's predicament was so awful that she fled to the desert. And yet Hagar—who was entirely vulnerable because she was a female, a servant, and a foreigner—is the first person in Scripture to name God.

READ Genesis 16:13-14.

What name does Hagar give God, and what does that name mean?

God saw Hagar, had compassion on her, and was present with her in her time of need. If you don't know all of Hagar's story, I would encourage you to read Genesis 16 when you have time. Hagar's story reminds us of God's grace and mercy, especially in our most vulnerable moments.

God saw Hagar, and God saw Naomi. And God sees you and me.

As you close your time today, I've included some prompts for prayer. You can write your prayers here or in a journal.

God, in this season of life,

I feel most seen when . . .

I feel invisible when . . .

I am carrying these heavy burdens . . .

God, thank you for carrying these burdens with me. Thank you for seeing me. Keep my heart from bitterness toward you and others. Amen.

DAY TWO • Moving Day

Let's explore a bit more today about when and where the book of Ruth takes place in the context of history and what instigated the family's initial move from Bethlehem to Moab.

READ Ruth 1:1-5 to refresh your memory.

What did you learn in these verses regarding the time period of the events we are reading about?

The book of Ruth occurred during the time of the judges (1375–1050 BC) after Joshua's death. If you have not read the book of Judges, it's a pretty rough period in the history of Israel—a time when "everyone did as they saw fit" (Judges 17:6). The nation experienced a repeated cycle of following God, forgetting God, doing some pretty terrible things and suffering the consequences, and then begging God for help. Over and over again. And it's within this context that we meet Ruth.

According to the first five verses of Ruth 1, why did Elimelek and Naomi initially move their family to the country of Moab?

In *Finding God in the Margins*, Carolyn Custis James calls Elimelek and Naomi and their sons "famine refugees." They left their home in Bethlehem in Judah and traveled about fifty miles to Moab seeking food. This would have been about a seven- to ten-days' journey on foot. In recent world history, we might liken their situation to the forty million people in Somalia, Ethiopia, and Kenya who faced a food crisis in 2023. This region suffered because of more than five years of drought, the impact of Covid-19, and the Russia-Ukraine war. The devastation was far reaching and many fled to other lands in search of food.

Moving is hard. Most of us will not have to flee our homes due to famine or war, but many of us have experienced the challenges that come with moving to a new location. If you've ever had to box up all your belongings and move to a new house, apartment, dorm room, city, or even a new country, then you know what I'm talking about. There's the physical work of packing up everything—your clothes, furniture, books, and perhaps decor—and then there's the emotional work of leaving a place that might hold memories.

I've moved probably a dozen times in my life. I still remember when I was eighteen and made my first big solo move from my parents' house in Chicago to my first dorm room in Grand Rapids, Michigan. It felt like a big deal to venture out on my own and discover life with roommates who were not family members.

I've made some even farther moves, like when I moved to Costa Rica for a semester in college or when my husband Ericlee and I first moved our family from California to Haiti to help direct a nonprofit organization.

My hardest move was a short move across town after Ericlee graduated to heaven. My daughters and I stayed in the house where he died for almost a year before I took the big step to buy a new house. Sorting, purging, and packing up all of our things from more than a decade of marriage was difficult. I cried a lot of tears as I left that home on Harrison Street full of so many memories—both good and hard.

Think of the moves you have experienced. What were the challenges of moving somewhere new?

Let's take a moment to go back to the beginning of Israel's history, which also involved a couple making a huge move. Read Genesis 12:1-8. This takes us all the way back to when God called Abram to pick up and move his family and follow him. God makes some important promises to Abram in this passage.

What are the three main promises God makes to Abram?

The promises listed here are known as the Abrahamic covenant. A covenant in the Bible is a promise made between two parties that is grounded in a relationship of trust and commitment. God made these promises so that Abram would trust and follow him. God also established the expectation that Abram and his family would follow his leading and commands.

The difference between Abram and Elimelek is that God *called* Abram to move with his family. We don't see any evidence that Elimelek was following God when he moved to Moab in search of provision. Let's pay attention to how this detail changes the course of Elimelek's life and his family's future.

The book of Ruth helps us explore themes such as displacement and homelessness. Ruth also illuminates finding hope in a foreign land and finding peace in the unexpected, unwanted, and unplanned. In fact, the book of Ruth reminds us of God's unfailing faithfulness to his people, and the remarkable love of a Redeemer.

READ Ruth 1:6-7.

These verses hold a sliver of hope that causes Naomi to make a life-altering choice. What key piece of news does Naomi hear in the fields of Moab? What does she decide to do?

Change can be hard, especially when it requires a move. We must grieve the past before we can step into the future. Sometimes change can also bring new opportunities and uncover new solutions we might not have imagined in our previous predicament.

Friend, no matter what challenges and change you are facing today, hold on to hope. Let the book of Ruth be an invitation and encouragement to you that God is always working behind the scenes on your behalf. Pray this prayer with me:

Dear Lord,

I am grieving . . .
As I acknowledge these things, I pray for healing.
I trust you with the present and the future.
Help me to hold on to hope and see the ways you are at work in my life and in the world.

Amen.

DAY THREE • From the Wrong Side of the Tracks

A few years ago, we took the family to go see the new movie version of *West Side Story*. This has been one of my favorite musicals for a long time. I've seen it various times on the stage and the different movie versions. The story is set in the mid-1950s in the Upper West Side of Manhattan in New York City. The musical depicts the rivalry between two street gangs, the Jets and the Sharks, who are warring for control of the neighborhood. The plot thickens when Tony, one of the Jets, falls in love with Maria, who is from the wrong side of the tracks, and whose brother, Bernardo, is the leader of the Sharks.

The 2021 movie version was a lot more gritty than other versions I've seen. It underscored the deep rivalry and violent fighting that ensued between these gangs. Because it is a modern adaptation of *Romeo and Juliet*, *West Side Story* also has a tragic ending. Despite all the festive dancing and music, viewers are left thinking about the social problems that led to such feuding between cultural groups. Although the context is vastly different, the book of Ruth is also a window into two contrasting cultures—the Moabites and Israelites—and what happened when they rubbed up next to each other.

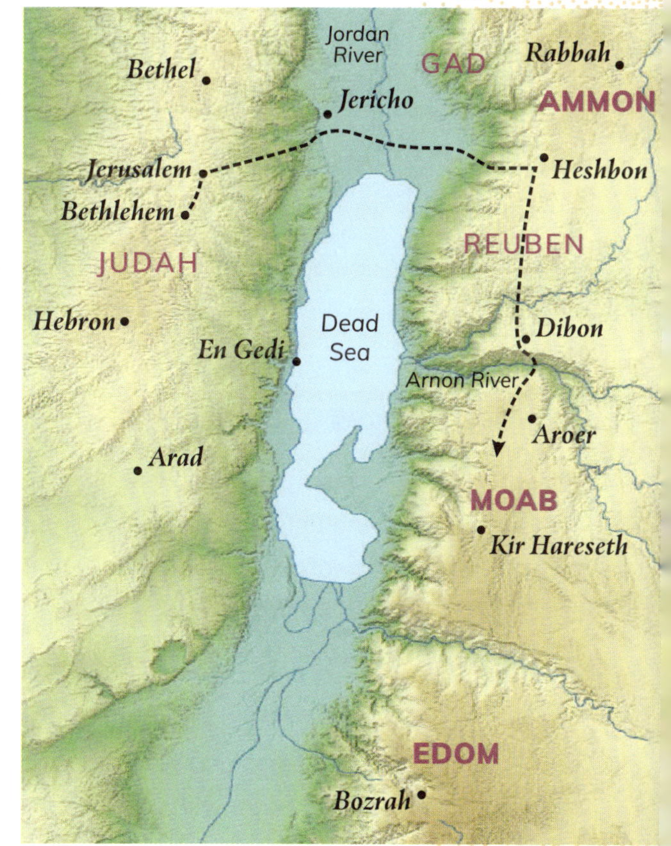

Take a few minutes to look at the map of this region. Note that the country of Moab was to the east of the Dead Sea (near modern-day Jordan), while the village of Bethlehem was situated in the region of Judah west of the Dead Sea. The sea served as the proverbial train tracks in this story. It would have been a long journey to travel from one side to the other.

The Israelites and the Moabites, like the Jets and Sharks, had a sordid history that began hundreds of years before the time of Ruth with Abraham's nephew Lot and his daughters. Lot traveled with Abraham to the Promised Land of Canaan. There came a point when the wealth of the two men—primarily livestock—became too much for the land to support. Abraham generously offered Lot first choice of the land. Lot chose the fertile Jordan Valley and settled in Sodom.

Eventually, God destroyed the city of Sodom because of the rampant sin of the people there. Lot's wife disobeyed God and became a pillar of salt when she looked back on the city. Lot and his daughters fled to the hills of Zoar in fear. They had already witnessed the destruction of the city where they grew up and the death of their mother.

READ Genesis 19:30-38.

What happened with Lot and his daughters and how did they take matters into their own hands?

This was certainly not the way God intended to fulfill his promises and multiply his family. Lot's daughter had a son named Moab, which means the Moabites were descendants of that incestuous union between Lot and one of his daughters. Through history, the Moabites worshiped other gods and were hated by the Israelites.

Later, we read in the book of 1 Kings that King Solomon took wives from Moab and worshiped other gods with them, which eventually had huge ramifications on his kingdom.

READ 1 Kings 11:1-8, 11.

What specifics do you learn about Solomon's choices in this passage and what were the consequences?

Let's take note that God was most angry about Solomon's disobedience and choice to worship false idols with his numerous wives. Solomon's loyalty to God waned over time as he engaged in idol worship. He even goes so far as to build a high place for Chemosh, the god of Moab who demanded child sacrifice. This compromise cost Solomon the kingdom. The children of Israel were warned repeatedly against intermarrying and participating in these pagan practices. God required loyalty and faithfulness from his chosen people because he had a greater plan for bringing all of the nations to himself.

According to Ruth 1:2, Elimelek and Naomi were Ephrathites from Bethlehem in Judah. They were descendants of Ephraim, the second son of Joseph. As Hebrews, they were raised differently from their pagan Moabite counterparts. They worshiped Yahweh, the one true God, who cared about them in a personal way. We can only imagine how difficult it was for them to move to Moab and fit in with the locals.

Somehow, both of Naomi's sons marry Moabite women. We do not read any details in the text about how these marriages were arranged crossculturally. Naomi probably never imagined her beloved sons marrying Moabites, especially given the animosity between the two groups.

To add insult to injury, there is no mention of children or grandchildren in the ten years Naomi lived in Moab, so we can assume both Ruth and Orpah were childless. As author Carolyn Custis James explains in her book, *Finding God in the Margins*, "The fact that not a single pregnancy is mentioned within those ten years suggests a whole new layer of suffering afflicted this family. Given a woman's normal monthly menstrual cycle, Naomi endured with her daughters-in-law, Ruth and Orpah, as many as 240 increasingly agonizing disappointments."

Name a disappointment you experienced that dragged on for a season or even years. How has this disappointment affected your life or your heart?

Naomi suffered one loss after another. She was ripped from her hometown and community. She faced the deaths of her husband and two sons, which would have inflicted a terrible grief. But there were also secondary losses for Naomi. When the men in Naomi's life died (the primary loss), Naomi then lost her sense of security and income. In a patriarchal culture, this would have also been the end of Elimelek's line because there was no male to carry his name forward. So not only would Naomi have lost her status and security, but she tasted hunger, heartache, and hopelessness as a result. Naomi has been compared to Job in the Bible because of her profound losses.

We can think of secondary losses as dominoes, where one loss triggers another. The loss of a loved one, or even a relationship or a job, are difficult in and of themselves. But the effects of those losses often mean the end of dreams, ambitions, or opportunities. Perhaps feeling a loss of identity can be the most unnerving secondary loss we experience.

We all have seasons in our lives when we must face grief and loss. Like Job and Naomi, we have the choice to cling to hope or curse God. Tomorrow we will read more about how God nudges these women toward the path to hope. Take some time to think about some of the losses and secondary losses you have endured in your life. Naming our losses and offering them up to God can help provide a first step on the pathway to healing.

As you close your time today, here are some prompts for prayer with space for writing if you choose.

God, I realize as I look back on my life that I have endured several losses, including . . .

I have experienced some secondary losses too, like . . .

God, thank you for listening and caring about my losses. Open my eyes to ways I can move forward from my disappointments and losses. Lift my head and heart today so I do not allow them to taint my attitude. Amen.

DAY FOUR • The Gospel in Ruth

Imagine this scene with me like the opening to a movie. The movie director drops us right in the tension of this pivotal moment. Three widows have packed up all their belongings because Naomi heard there is food back in her homeland. After more than a decade of living as a famine refugee in Moab, Naomi is homeward bound.

The camera pans across the desert landscape to give us a view of Naomi and her two daughters-in-law on the dusty road leading back to Bethlehem. They are carrying all their belongings with them. The camera pulls in close to let viewers hear Naomi give Ruth and Orpah some passionate instructions.

READ Ruth 1:7-12.

Why might Naomi release her daughters-in-law to return to their Moabite families?

As you read verses 8 and 9, what is Naomi most concerned about?

Naomi made an immense sacrifice here. Culturally, her daughters-in-law were obligated to care for her. Yet she emancipated them to return to their families and stay in Moab. She seemed to want to spare the women further suffering. She knew the road to Bethlehem was long and offered little hope of redemption for these women who are incredibly vulnerable at this point.

The good news is God has a heart for the vulnerable. He identifies them, takes up their cause, and cares for them in creative ways. In his book *Generous Justice*, Timothy Keller explains how God has a tender heart for the "quartet of the vulnerable": the widow, the orphan, the foreigner, and the poor. Ruth and Orpah represent all four of these categories.

At a basic level, the vulnerable are without protection and susceptible to physical or emotional attack or harm. Keller writes that in premodern, agrarian societies like those described in the Bible, these four groups of people did not have any social power. They were just barely surviving in most cases, often hovering close to starvation. Today, vulnerable people groups include refugees, migrant workers, people experiencing homelessness, foster children, single parents, the elderly, and the undocumented. Many of the vulnerable included in these groups are women and children.

READ AND REFLECT on the following Scriptures. What do they reveal about God and his heart for the vulnerable?

> **Jeremiah 22:3 (ESV)—*"Thus says the Lord: Do justice and righteousness, and deliver from the hand of the oppressor him who has been robbed. And do no wrong or violence to the resident alien, the fatherless, and the widow, nor shed innocent blood in this place."***

James 1:27 (ESV)—"Religion that is pure and undefiled before God the Father is this: to visit orphans and widows in their affliction, and to keep oneself unstained from the world."

In Ruth 1:8-9, God's core character quality and his heart for the marginalized are revealed through the words of Naomi. Different translations include some nuances in the phrasing: "May the Lord *deal kindly* with you" (ESV); "May the Lord *show kindness* to you" (CSB); "May God *treat you as graciously* as" (MSG); "May the Lord *deal faithfully* with you" (CEB). The prominent word in these verses is the Hebrew word *hesed*. Although our English Bibles frequently translate this word as kindness, love, steadfast love, or lovingkindness, that's an oversimplification. It's difficult to translate hesed into a single English word because it embodies a cornucopia of concepts including mercy, loyalty, steadfast love, covenant faithfulness, extravagant generosity, *and* lovingkindness. God is our example of hesed. He embodies covenantal, unwavering, and unconditional love for us.

In his book *Inexpressible: Hesed and the Mystery of God's Lovingkindness*, Michael Card takes a deep dive into exploration of God's hesed. This word occurs nearly 250 times in the Hebrew Bible and "can open the door into an entire world—the world of God's own heart, the world of loving our neighbor and perhaps even our enemies."

Naomi offered her daughters-in-law a blessing of God's hesed and rest in these verses. When Naomi urged her daughters-in-law to turn back, she kissed them and the women wept loudly together. We get a glimpse of their deep bond and love for each other. These women navigated years of grief together. In verse ten, both women refused to go back. They wanted to accompany Naomi to Bethlehem.

When I read these words, I thought about my own grief journey in losing my husband and how it has bonded me to certain people who were present with me or who have experienced similar things.

Think of a time where you faced a season of challenge, grief, loss, or disappointment. Who stayed with you throughout that season? And what did their willingness to stay with you reveal about them?

After offering her blessing, Naomi got pragmatic.

READ Ruth 1:12-17, paying close attention to Naomi's convincing words to Ruth and Orpah. What is Naomi's argument for why the young widows should stay in Moab? How do the two women respond?

Orpah heeded her mother-in-law's advice and chose to return home. She took a more sensible approach, while Ruth took a courageous risk. Ruth's passionate response included these often-quoted words: "Don't urge me to leave you or to turn back from you. Where you go I will go, and where you stay I will stay. Your people will be my people and your God my God. Where you die I will die, and there I will be buried. May the LORD deal with me, be it ever so severely, if even death separates you and me" (Ruth 1:16-17).

Ruth stood at the fork in the road and decided to follow Naomi and Naomi's God—Yahweh. She walked away from her home in Moab, her family of origin, and her past. On the road to Bethlehem, Ruth's life is transformed. In Hebrew, Bethlehem means the "house of bread"—a symbol of provision. Ruth didn't know it at the time, but trusting in Yahweh, Naomi's God, meant walking toward provision, freedom, and eventually unexpected redemption for both her and Naomi. This was just the beginning of a new chapter for both women.

Friend, if are feeling hopeless, remember Ruth. If you are wading through a messy season feeling like redemption is out of reach, remember how Yahweh met Ruth on the road to Bethlehem. He met me there too.

Ruth's story invites all of us to meet with God, who is the greatest provider and comforter.

Maybe you had a dramatic moment of decision like Ruth. Or perhaps your feelings about following God have grown little by little over time. Even if you're undecided, write out a prayer to him now, letting him know how you feel or any questions you might have. If you haven't met with God before, it's never too late, my friend.

Dear God,

I am feeling . . .

I still have questions about . . .

I do desire to follow you and discover the redemption you have for my life.

Amen.

DAY FIVE • Reflect

ART AND JOURNALING PRACTICE

For the past four days we have been digging through the details of the first chapter of the book of Ruth. Today you are invited to take time to slow down, meditate, and reflect. Meditating on Scripture and taking time to respond is an important practice. Give yourself time to look over the chapter and the notes from the last four days. Let the Scriptures we have studied sink in.

Is there a verse or truth you learned this week that was meaningful to you? Write it out below. How does it apply to you today in your present season?

Take some time to look at this beautiful piece of art designed by Octavia Mingerink. This might feel uncomfortable at first, but linger awhile.

Describe the woman you see in the illustration.

What does this illustration say to you about grief?

We are all affected by grief at various times in life because we are all affected by loss. If you are grieving something in your life, bring it to Jesus' feet. Write about what you are processing today below or in a journal.

The book of Ruth invites us to process our grief and grapple with our theology of suffering. Our "theology" is what we believe about a topic as it relates to God. Naomi struggled because of all the loss and heartache she faced in her life. And yet, the God of *hesed* love does not operate that way. When we are suffering, we may forget what we know to be true about God.

One of my favorite bands of all time is U2. In 2015, I had the opportunity to go to a U2 concert at the Forum in Los Angeles. A friend and I scored general admission tickets, which meant we were standing right in front of the stage. That night U2 sang many of their iconic songs that have topped the charts through the years, but my favorite is still a song titled "40" that uses words straight from Psalm 40 written by the shepherd boy David. The song "40" is for those who are waiting, for those who are wandering and wondering, for those who are longing for a redemption story.

Now let's read through Psalm 40 in **The Message** version. If you don't have a print copy, you can find it online.

Take some time to journal here about how this psalm meets you in your place of need today. Share with God about what you are waiting for and how you are feeling in the waiting.

WEEK TWO

The Meeting

RUTH 2:1-13

GROUP SESSION: THE MEETING

Sometimes we use the word *providence* to refer to the protective or spiritual care of God over his people. This is far different from popular phrases in American culture like *as luck would have it* or *in the cards for me* or *good karma*. More recent slang may even include something like this: "It was so random, but *this* happened to me today . . ." None of these responses specifically point to the work of God to guide and care for humans.

In today's video, I share about some of the "just so happens" parts in my story and Ruth's story. Let's take some time in our groups today to talk about how God is often working behind the scenes to bring together details in our stories. It's more than happenstance. He cares about our good and his glory.

WATCH

Take some time now to **WATCH** the video that accompanies the week two study.

READ

READ Ruth 2:1-13.

DISCUSS

1. **How would you describe a "just so happens" story? If you know of such an experience, what was the most surprising aspect for you?**

2. How would you describe the kind of provision Ruth (and Naomi) received in Ruth 2:1-13?

3. Tell about a time when God provided for you and your family in a surprising way. How did that make you feel?

4. READ the following passages aloud. What do you learn about widows and their plight or challenges in Bible times?

1 Kings 17:7-16

Mark 12:38-44

Acts 9:36-42

5. How was God working behind the scenes in the lives of these widows and providing for them in unique ways?

6. How has God used their stories to minister to others?

7. What are some of the ways your church or your community cares for widows? If nothing comes to mind, is there something you might suggest or initiate?

8. READ James 1:17. What does this verse show about God and how does this relate to what you have discussed today about God's provision?

PRAY

As you close your time, here are a few suggestions to guide you in prayer together:

- Thank God for the surprising ways he continues to weave together details to care for us in personal ways.
- If you have a "just so happens" story, call out to him in gratitude with your group.
- Ask God to provide for the widows in your community.
- Sometimes we see the marginalized and vulnerable around us as "less than" or not contributing to community. Pray against any attitudes like this in your own heart and invite God to show you the value of the people in your midst.

If you prefer, you can write out a prayer in the margin or in a journal.

MEMORY VERSE

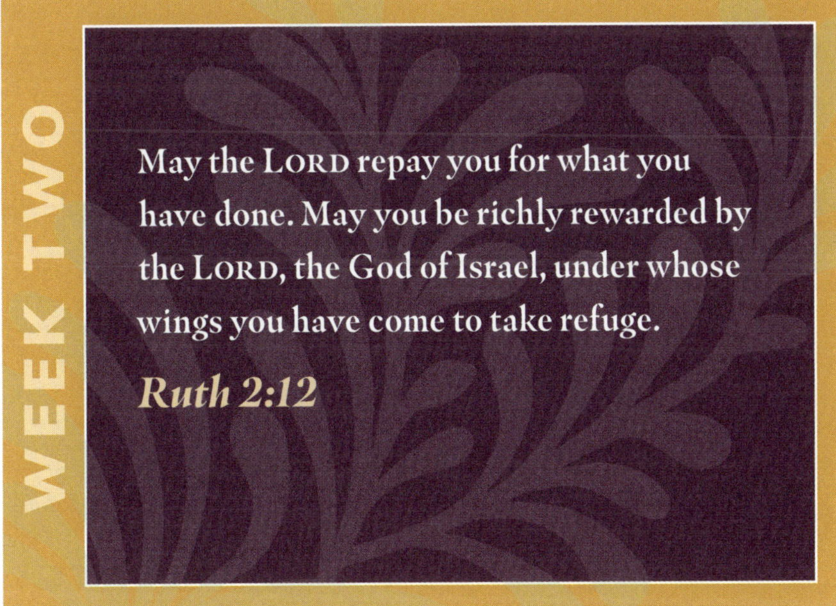

DAY ONE • God's Unexpected Provision

My daughter took a video production class in high school for a few years in a row. The first assignment her teacher gave her was to study and film a subject from different angles. Some of the angles included: bird's eye view, medium shot, close-up, wide shot, worm's eye view, point of view, and extra-wide shot. As I watched her learning to use different camera angles, it got me thinking about how important it is for us to examine every story of the Bible from different angles too.

Last week we considered the cultural context and Naomi's perspective and predicament in the book of Ruth. This week we are going to look at the story more from Ruth's point of view. Ruth is our lead character in chapter two. She has just pledged her allegiance to Yahweh, the God of Israel, and followed her mother-in-law Naomi around the Dead Sea through the land of Judah and into the town of Bethlehem.

God is reclaiming Ruth as his daughter through the unfolding events in her life. In much the same way that God parted the Red Sea for the Israelites so they could escape slavery in Egypt, God opens a passage to provision for Ruth. She must step out in courage and overcome some of the prejudice that precedes her in Bethlehem.

READ Ruth 2:1-13.

What do you note about Ruth and her personality through her words and actions in this section? How would you describe her to a friend?

Ruth arrived in Bethlehem as a foreigner (a Moabite), an immigrant, a famine refugee, and a young widow. These are some of the different angles or categories others put her in. Each one came with its own stigma and challenges.

In week one, day three, we learned about the animosity between the Moabites and the Jews. Ruth immigrated from Moab into a mostly homogeneous Jewish town. People would have noticed she was different—from her dark skin tone to her shabby, foreign dress to her accent.

If you have ever felt like an outsider in a situation, describe the emotions that you experienced in that setting.

Ruth also does not know the nuances of the culture. Because she and Naomi need food, Ruth boldly steps into the Jewish welfare system.

READ Leviticus 19:9-10 and Deuteronomy 24:17-22.

How do you understand the provision for the poor and needy, according to these laws?

This Jewish welfare system basically designated the leftovers or the surplus in the fields for the poor. As Carolyn Custis James describes in *The Gospel of Ruth*, when harvesting a field, like the one Boaz owned, hired men would go through first, grabbing handfuls of grain and cutting them off at the base. Then the female workers followed to gather and bind the cut grain. The gleaners were allowed to go through last and pick up whatever leftovers remained after the hired men and women had completed their work. By the honor system, landowners would carry out these laws.

Gleaning was considered a shameful way to live. It was also precarious, particularly for women, who faced danger from other hungry gleaners scrambling for the leftovers or at the hands of the hired harvesters who might take advantage of them while away from others in the field.

According to Ruth 2:7, Ruth had asked for permission to glean from the field, following the reapers. Let's look at why Ruth's request was a little out of the ordinary. Ruth bypassed the customary protocol for gleaning on the edges of the field and requested something more.

Why do you think this detail was included? What does it reveal to us about Ruth?

When Boaz returned home, he noticed Ruth. As mentioned before, she had some things that definitely would have made her stick out in this crowd. After Boaz hears from his foreman a bit about Ruth's story, he goes to talk to her. He answers her courageous request to glean among the sheaves with an unexpected grace and generosity. He easily could have refused her, but he doesn't. Ruth is not motivated by greed but by giving. Reread Ruth 2:8-9.

What does Boaz offer Ruth in these verses and why are they significant in her situation?

In this section of Ruth, we begin to see God's plans for provision unfold. Even though we do not see God mentioned in the text, Ruth gets to experience how he is working on behalf of her and Naomi.

Let's pray about a time when you weren't able to see God working until you looked back over past events.

Dear God,

Remember when ________________ happened? I was so blessed. And as I thought about it, you allowed ________________ and ________________ to happen to make it possible! Thank you for being there in the details, even when I'm not aware of it at the time.

DAY TWO • Woman of Valor

In this section of Ruth, we get a window into Ruth's character. Ruth is vulnerable in her position as a woman, a widow of little means, and a foreigner. She also is a woman of integrity who displays incredible resilience. Ruth is proactive, a risk taker, ready to work hard, and brimming with courage. Ruth may be a poor, barren, young widow, but she is certainly not the picture of a demure or passive woman following her mother-in-law to Bethlehem like a lost puppy.

Let's take note of how Ruth responds to Boaz when they meet.

READ Ruth 2:10-13.

What is Ruth's physical posture in this moment? What might this reveal about her "heart" posture?

Let's take a look at Proverbs 31, a poem about wisdom and womanly excellence. It was written as an acrostic poem with each verse beginning with successive letters of the Hebrew alphabet. Bearing this in mind, read Proverbs 31:10-31.

What is the heart attitude of the Proverbs 31 woman? How does this shape the way she lives?

Go back and underline or note all the character qualities used to describe "women of wisdom" in Proverbs 31. What are some of the character qualities described in this poem that remind you of Ruth and her character?

Ruth is a woman of valor like the woman described in Proverbs 31. The poem is less a checklist and more a celebration of how God designed women in beautiful, diverse ways.

The central theme of Proverbs and the poem is reiterated near the end: "a woman who fears the LORD will be greatly praised" (Proverbs 31:30 NLT). Fear of the Lord is not a negative thing. The fear of the Lord is a deep respect and reverence for God and his ways. It's holding in our hearts both his great power *and* his generous mercy toward us. And as Psalm 111:10 tells us, "The fear of the LORD is the beginning of wisdom."

The phrase "woman of valor," or *eshet khayil* (EY-shet CHAH-yeel) in Hebrew, is used by Jewish women to cheer one another on. This phrase or blessing is said in celebration of everything from promotions to pregnancies to acts of mercy and justice to battles with cancer—a hearty, "*eshet khayil*"! (Think of it as something like a Jewish "You go, girl!") Jewish men are the ones who more often memorize Proverbs 31 and sing it as a song of praise to the ladies in their lives. In fact, it is traditionally sung at the beginning of the Shabbat meal on Friday evenings.

What is extraordinary in this story is that Ruth is not a "good, Hebrew wife" who has grown up in the religious culture. She was raised a

Moabite and then grafted into Naomi's Jewish family through Naomi's son, while living in Moab. She comes to know Yahweh—Naomi's God—as an adult.

And yet Ruth, an outsider in this culture, walks with courage and kindness like a woman of valor. She disrupts the narrative of the day about outsiders, specifically Moabites. Ruth is welcomed by Boaz to the center of the field to glean. She is honored and praised because she is a woman with a servant's heart and the fear of the Lord.

It's interesting to note that in the Christian Bible, the book of Ruth follows the book of Judges, since Ruth lived "in the days when the judges ruled" (Ruth 1:1). But in the Hebrew Bible, the book of Ruth follows the book of Proverbs, setting up Ruth as an example of a woman of valor.

Theologian Carolyn Custis Jones in *The Gospel of Ruth* describes Ruth this way: "Her [Ruth's] loyalty to Yahweh prompts her to challenge the religious status quo and lead others into a whole new realm of allegiance to Yahweh that carries early hints of the teachings of Jesus. . . . Ruth embodies the utter difference the gospel makes in us and in our relationships with others—generations before Jesus was born."

Is there an area in your life where you desire to be more kind and courageous? How could Ruth inspire you?

Friend, may we be encouraged and challenged by Ruth and her posture in the face of adversity.

Lord, our Provider, see my words above and give me more courage and kindness as I serve you in the field where I am, where you have made a place for me.

DAY THREE • A Worthy Man

Whenever I'm reading a book or watching a movie, it's always exciting when a new character is introduced. In Ruth 2, we meet Boaz. The narrator takes time to underscore a few things about Boaz before he actually shows up in the scene.

READ Ruth 2:1 in a few different translations. *(You can use a website like BibleGateway.com or BibleStudyTools.com to look at different translations of the Bible, or use the YouVersion Bible App on your phone.)*

What does this one verse tell us about Boaz?

Boaz was called a "man of standing" (NIV) or a "worthy man" (ESV)—someone we can infer was connected with wealth, influence, and power. Boaz was well-known in his community, a landowner and leader. The Hebrew word used here is *ish gibbor khayil*. Sound familiar? This echoes the word used to describe Ruth in our study yesterday, *eshet khayil*.

Other men "of standing" mentioned in the Bible were Gideon, Jepthah, and Naaman, who were mighty men of war. This might indicate that

Boaz was an experienced warrior in addition to being wealthy. However, we do not get the sense that Boaz is strutting his stuff when he arrives. In fact, his response to Ruth gleaning in his field reveals a different side of his character.

REREAD Ruth 2:4.

What is the first phrase that spilled from Boaz's mouth when he arrived at his field? What does this tell you about him?

Let's keep reading carefully to learn more about Boaz.

READ Ruth 2:8-11.

What are some of your observations about the way Boaz treats Ruth when he meets her?

Boaz's only obligation is to offer this foreigner the leftovers from his field, but his kind generosity shines in this moment. His immediate response is a tender word to Ruth that goes above and beyond obligation and cultural norms.

If we do a little digging through Scripture, we discover that Boaz's mother was Rahab, who played an important role in the book of Joshua. Joshua was Moses' protégé. After Moses' death, God commissioned Joshua to lead the next generation of Israelites into the Promised Land. Joshua sent two men to scope out the land in Jericho. Rahab, who is noted in Scripture as a Canaanite prostitute, helps protect them in a strategic way.

Let's take some time to learn about Boaz's mama so we can deepen our understanding of her son.

READ Joshua 2:1-16.

What kind of woman was Rahab ? How was she courageous and helpful to the spies?

What do we learn about Rahab's faith in Yahweh?

Joshua 6:25 (NASB) details how Rahab and her family were saved: "However, Rahab the prostitute and her father's household and all she had, Joshua spared; and she has lived in the midst of Israel to this day, because she hid the messengers whom Joshua sent to spy out Jericho." Rahab was a foreigner who had been invited into God's family because she trusted the God of Israel and showed kindness to his people.

They say the apple doesn't fall far from the tree. We can imagine that Boaz grew up with stories passed down from his mama about helping the Israelite spies. Some commentators believe his daddy Salmon was one of those original spies Rahab saved, and in turn he saved her and her family. Rahab also would have understood in a personal way what it felt like being an outsider who became an insider. We can guess that she modeled for Boaz compassion for the foreigner, since she was a Canaanite living among the Israelites.

Also, Rahab's faith is praised twice in the New Testament:

> By faith the prostitute Rahab did not perish along with those who were disobedient, after she had welcomed the spies in peace. (Hebrews 11:31 NASB)
>
> In the same way, was Rahab the prostitute not justified by works also when she received the messengers and sent them out by another way? (James 2:25 NASB).

Rahab's faith put into action is remembered for generations. In the book of Ruth, we see how Boaz continued his mother's legacy. Boaz proved to be a man of faith and generosity. He noticed Ruth not for her beauty or glass slippers but because of her courage and kindness.

How does Boaz affirm or admire Ruth in Ruth 2:8-11?

Although many try to read romance into this story, Boaz's words remind us what he truly valued. He was impressed with Ruth's bravery to leave her homeland in order to care for Naomi. He admired her courage and kindness. He blessed her, asking God to repay her for what she'd sacrificed. The irony and the beauty is that Boaz himself becomes those wings of protection, offering Ruth comfort and refuge in his very own field.

Ruth's honest and emotional response tells us that she is overcome by the generosity that Boaz would offer to her—a foreigner: "Oh sir, such grace, such kindness—I don't deserve it. You've touched my heart, treated me like one of your own. And I don't even belong here!'" (Ruth 2:13 MSG).

Through this exchange between Boaz and Ruth, it's beautiful to see how God had been working all along. Maybe you find yourself at the edge of a field today feeling like you are stuck with the leftovers. Take heart, God is right there with you. He offers the most unexpected provision if we are willing to lift our eyes and look for it.

God of Rahab and of Ruth, you see the places where it seems as if only leftovers remain for me. Thank you for being with me, and open my eyes to the small and great ways you provide for me. Amen.

DAY FOUR • God's Heart for Widows

God's heart for vulnerable groups is threaded throughout the Bible. Verse after verse, chapter after chapter in the Old and New Testaments reveal God's compassion, mercy, grace, and love for those who are marginalized. Deuteronomy 10:18 offers an example of his heart: "He defends the cause of the fatherless and the widow, and loves the foreigner residing among you, giving them food and clothing." He is a defender and lover. From Hagar to Hannah, from Rahab to Ruth, we also see how God specifically cared about marginalized women. God provided for these women in personal ways and empowered them to minister to others.

One widow God used mightily in ministry is the widow of Zarephath, who fed the Old Testament prophet Elijah in a time of need. Elijah ministered in the northern kingdom of Israel and represented God in a showdown against the wicked King Ahab and his wife, Jezebel, who worshiped Baal. But before Elijah confronted Ahab, God sent him to Zarephath to have a meal with a widow.

READ 1 Kings 17:8-16 to learn more about her story.

How would you describe the widow and her attitude in this passage?

What does Elijah do for her? How is this an example of God's creative provision for her and her family?

First Kings 17:15 is a powerful moment for the widow of Zarephath. Because of her obedience, she receives God's unexpected provision. She and her family were on the brink of starvation, but God uses her to feed his prophet and meets her in her lack.

I studied many of these passages about God's heart for widows and orphans with my late husband, Ericlee. As a couple, God specifically gave us a heart for orphans. We helped start two children's homes in Haiti and through the years provided support to many friends who adopted children. We even pursued plans to adopt children of our own before Ericlee went to heaven.

I didn't know I would need these same Scriptures to affirm and encourage me years later when I stood at my husband's graveside at age thirty-seven as a widow. In my twenties, God moved my heart with compassion for orphans, but in my thirties he gave me compassion for another vulnerable group mentioned in those same Scriptures—widows.

Grief can be a lonely journey, especially when you are caring for young children still at home. I am deeply grateful for the multitiered community of support I had after my husband's death. My daughters and I received generous support from several churches and many outside the church. They brought us meals, helped with our medical bills, invited us to visit, sent cards, and most importantly, were present with us through the darkest days of grief. We also had our Haitian friends who had become family through the years. They prayed over us and loved us from afar. I was humbled again and again by God's special provision for us through his people.

In 2 Corinthians 1:3-4, the apostle Paul wrote about the ways God can use our grief: "Praise be to the God and Father of our Lord Jesus Christ, the Father of compassion and the God of all comfort, who comforts us in all our troubles, so that we can comfort those in any trouble with the comfort we ourselves receive from God." Did you catch that? *We can offer comfort to others because we ourselves have experienced comfort from God.*

Comfort is one of the specific things Ruth thanks Boaz for in Ruth 2:13. We know Ruth's history. She was childless for more than a decade of marriage. Her father-in-law died, and then she lost her husband and brother-in-law. This woman has endured grief upon grief. When Boaz speaks kindly to her, Ruth feels a sense of comfort she has not felt in a long time—*if ever.*

Write about a time when you have received comfort or kindness from someone in your life. How has that experience affected the way you comfort others?

Over time, God began to open doors for me to share my story and help those navigating grief, especially other widows. I quickly discovered that many did not have the kind of community support I had received. This burdened my heart, and I began to pray for creative ways I might bridge this gap for widows.

After praying for almost a year, I launched the Widow Mama Collective on Facebook, an online support group for widows who are mothering children at home. Three other widow mamas who are also writers joined me to help create a safe space where widows might share their experiences with grief, their questions about parenting, and their prayer requests on the journey. The group continues today with more than six hundred members.

There's a proverb in several cultures that says, "Grief shared is half grief; joy shared is double joy." My experience is that grief feels less heavy when we share it with one another. When we show compassion and care for people who are grieving, we are multiplying the comfort Jesus Christ first offered us through his life and love.

Friend, I want to challenge you today to think about anyone in your midst who is grieving—widows, widowers, orphans, childless parents, divorcées, caregivers, and others. As believers, we are called to walk alongside all who grieve. We have an opportunity to be Immanuel—God with us—to them.

How might you offer comfort to someone grieving in your circle or community today? What is one concrete step you could take?

If you are the friend who is grieving, I want you to know that God sees you and hears you in this season. Ask the Lord to show you one person you could reach out to, even if it's for a small, simple thing.

DAY FIVE • Reflect

ART AND JOURNALING PRACTICE

The last four days we have been treasure hunting through the first thirteen verses of the second chapter of the book of Ruth. Today you are invited to take time to slow down, meditate, and reflect. Meditating on Scripture and taking time to respond are important practices.

Give yourself time to look over the chapter and the notes from the last four days. Let the Scriptures we have studied sink in.

Is there a verse or truth you learned this week that was meaningful to you? Write it out below. How does it apply to you in your present season?

Take some time to look at this beautiful piece of art. I want to encourage you to linger with it awhile. Observe the colors, the curves and edges, the details.

What do you see in this artwork?

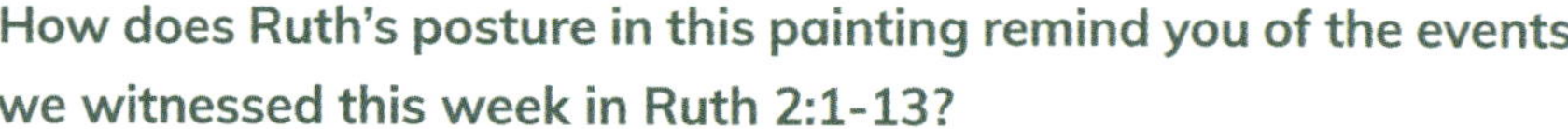

How does Ruth's posture in this painting remind you of the events we witnessed this week in Ruth 2:1-13?

What might the Holy Spirit be speaking to you today through this piece of art?

In Ruth 2:12 (NLT), Boaz uses imagery that echoes throughout the Scriptures, particularly in the Psalms: "May the Lord, the God of Israel, under whose wings you have come to take refuge, reward you fully for what you have done." The idea of God being like a mother bird who shelters her babies under her wings is powerful.

READ through and meditate on Psalm 91 in the New Living Translation, if possible.

What verses, phrases, or images speak to you?

As you consider how Ruth received protection and provision under God's wings, think about ways that God has protected and provided for you.

As you conclude, use the language of Psalm 91 to guide you in your prayer.

> *God, I thank you for being a shelter, a refuge, a place of safety, the giver of rest . . .*
>
> *God, I need your protection, your covering, your rescue . . .*
>
> *God, thank you for your promise, "When you call on me, I will answer."*
>
> *Amen.*

WEEK THREE

Feast or Famine?

RUTH 2:14-23

GROUP SESSION: FACING THE UNEXPECTED

When I read my wedding vows to my beloved Ericlee, the thought never entered my mind that I would be widowed before the age of forty. I didn't imagine I would be navigating grief with my three young daughters eleven years after we married. So often life brings us challenges that are disorienting. Maybe you can relate. And yet, in the midst of unexpected tragedy and grief, God so often meets us with his presence.

In this week's video, I unfold the unexpected story of how God brought Shawn into my life and how our relationship pivoted from platonic to romantic.

Let's take some time in our groups to talk about how God is the Master Author who often surprises us with the unexpected plot twist.

WATCH

Take some time now to **WATCH** the video that accompanies the week three study.

READ

READ Ruth 2:14-23.

DISCUSS

1. **What are some ways that Boaz showed generosity toward Ruth and Naomi in these verses?**

2. **How would you describe Naomi's reaction after Ruth returned from her first day of gleaning?**

3. **What aspect of your life story feels unexpected or surprising?**

4. How have your unexpected experiences shaped you as a person?

As we've been learning, one of the significant themes in the book of Ruth is God's *hesed*. Michael Card in *Inexpressible* describes hesed this way: "This small three-letter word [in Hebrew script] seems to always be there when the door is open from one life to another, when the unexpected and undeserved gift of one's life is offered with no strings attached, when inexpressible acts of adoption, forgiveness, and courage occur that leave us speechless."

READ the following Scriptures and notice the different words and phrases that are used to express hesed in English (italics mine in each passage):

> Then the Lord passed in front of him and proclaimed:
>
> Yahweh—Yahweh is a compassionate and gracious God, slow to anger and rich in *faithful love* [hesed] and truth, maintaining *faithful love* [hesed] to a thousand generations, forgiving wrongdoing, rebellion, and sin. But He will not leave the guilty unpunished, bringing the consequences of the fathers' wrongdoing on the children and grandchildren to the third and fourth generation. (Exodus 34:6-7 HCSB)

You gave me life and showed me *kindness* [hesed], and in your providence watched over my spirit. (Job 10:12)

Surely your goodness and *love* [hesed] will follow me all the days of my life, and I will dwell in the house of the LORD forever. (Psalm 23:6)

5. **If you think of other examples in the Bible that display God's hesed, list them below and share them with your group.**

6. **READ Ruth 2:20 in *The Message* version: "Naomi said to her daughter-in-law, 'Why, GOD bless that man! GOD hasn't quite walked out on us after all! He still loves us, in bad times as well as good!'" How does this version highlight Naomi's attitude toward the situation and God?**

PRAY

In this week's video, I shared about how I was comforted by Shawn's generosity, and how Ruth was comforted by Boaz's generosity. Who has been generous or brought you comfort in your life?

As we conclude with prayer, let's express our gratitude to God
for placing these people in our lives . . .
for the kindness these people have shown us . . .
and that God sees us—in difficult times as well as in good times.

Father, we are grateful for the many ways you have provided for us. Today we are reminded of and warmed by the generosity and kindness shown to us by others, and how their love for us is a reflection of your love. Thank you for your goodness and love that will follow us all the days of our lives. Amen.

MEMORY VERSE

DAY ONE • Sharing a Meal

I'm a foodie, and the way to my heart is definitely through my stomach. I grew up in the kitchen with my mama and grandmas and aunties. My mama let me stir the ruby red ragù in the pot and help her stuff pasta shells with ricotta cheese. Grandma Cora made me her helper when she was rolling *lumpia* and adding ingredients to her *pancit*. Now I love cooking with my daughters and trying out new restaurants with my family and friends. When we share a meal with someone—however elaborate or simple—there is an intimate and personal connection that often happens. This is why Jesus often chose to minister to people at the table.

Today we are going to take some time to reflect on the very important role food plays in the book of Ruth and the growing relationship between Boaz, our hero, and Ruth, our heroine.

READ Ruth 2:14-17.

What are some things you observe about this first meal that Ruth and Boaz share? Where are they? What are they eating and how does it create connection between them?

My favorite local restaurant in central California where I live is a place called Heirloom, which showcases local, seasonal produce and creative dishes. I could eat there every day of the week and have something different each time. As I was reading this section of Ruth, I kept thinking about this delicious appetizer they make at Heirloom called

Loom bread, which is like a cross between flatbread and a croissant. It's light and flaky, and melts in your mouth when served with Brie cheese and fig jam. My mouth is watering just thinking about it.

Can you imagine Boaz inviting Ruth to the table to share a Loom bread and Brie appetizer? Or maybe it was closer to pita bread and balsamic vinegar? Keep in mind Ruth's situation. She had grown accustomed to hunger pangs. Ruth and Naomi left Moab because they were homeless and without resources. They traveled the distance because they heard there was a harvest in Bethlehem, which could mean more food—or at least *some* food—for these widows.

When Boaz leaned over to Ruth at lunch break and says these words, "Come over here, and help yourself to some food. You can dip your bread in the sour wine" (Ruth 2:14 NLT), it's an invitation to a feast.

The passage tells us Ruth ate until she was satisfied. She savored every morsel of that bread dipped in wine vinegar. Imagine the contrast. Ruth came to the field of Boaz to glean—basically to gather up the scraps—but now she is being invited to the table with the field owner and his workers. Boaz offered her a portion of his own food. This would not be common, for gleaners to be included this way. In fact, it probably wasn't common for the landowner to come and eat among his own workers either. But Boaz was a different kind of boss.

Can you think of the most amazing meal you have ever tasted? What about that meal made it special?

For Ruth, this was probably top of her list for best meal ever. There are even leftovers, which Boaz later urges her to take home in a to-go box, along with the grain she has gathered. Theologian Iain Duguid in *Esther and Ruth* illuminates Ruth's situation: "The joy of having enough to eat is a hard concept for us to grasp in our affluence, for we are used to satisfying our appetites three times a day, with snacks in between. But for a foreign widow to be able to eat to the point where she was full and still have some left over to take home . . . what a feast!"

The English Standard Version says Ruth "ate until she was satisfied" (Ruth 2:14). Ruth 2:18 ESV also emphasizes how Ruth was satisfied: "She also brought out and gave her what food she had left over after being satisfied." The repetition of that word satisfied is important here. In Latin cultures, someone pushes back from the table after a big meal and says, "*Estoy satisfecha*" in Spanish to indicate they are full and satisfied. This is also a compliment to the host or cook. Ruth feasted on abundant food but also experienced abundant generosity.

REREAD Ruth 2:11-12.

How does Boaz call out Ruth's generosity toward her mother-in-law?

Boaz responds to Ruth's actions with like actions. MAKE A LIST of all the ways Boaz shows Ruth generosity in Ruth 2:14-21. How is Boaz modeling kindness that goes above and beyond the expected compassion extended to widows?

Boaz offered Ruth abundant food and water. He urged her to draw water from the jars his men have filled. That means she doesn't have to go carry water from the well herself. In Ruth 2:15-17, she is invited to gather grain from the bundles the harvesters have already gathered. That means she is given food that she did not earn. Then she returned home to share this abundance with her mother-in-law Naomi, who is overjoyed by God's provision.

The generosity of this meal provided by Boaz is a preview of sorts that points to the many instances that Jesus invited outsiders to the table. He was known for dining with tax collectors, fishermen, and marginalized women, both Jews and Gentiles. He invited everyone to his table to feast on the grace served up by his Father.

Take some time to read the story in John 6:1-14 about how Jesus used a boy's lunch to feed five thousand–plus people.

What does this story reveal about God's generosity and abundance?

In what ways is this Gospel story similar to Ruth's experience?

Write out a prayer below, thanking God for the ways he has been generous and shown you abundance.

DAY TWO • The Dignity of Work

Today we are going to continue with a close reading of Ruth 2:15-17. Read the text again. Notice how Boaz invited Ruth to work. He offered both protection and opportunity, but he didn't do all the work for her. He extended kindness and mercy, which honored her. Then he opened his field for her to gather food for herself.

What instructions does Boaz give his men about letting Ruth glean? How are these a measure of both protection and dignity?

Through Ruth's trust in God and her willingness to work, she experienced God's abundance. We learn that Ruth collected an *ephah* of barley, which Iain Duguid in *Esther and Ruth* explains was somewhere between thirty and fifty pounds of grain, capable of producing 672 slices of whole grain bread. We are talking food for several weeks.

What do you imagine Ruth was thinking as she hauled that barley home to Naomi? How does this help you better understand Ruth's situation?

Let's go back to Genesis and think about how God designed humans for creativity and work.

READ the following passages. What hints do these verses give us about God's design for humans and work?

Genesis 1:26-28

Genesis 2:15

Genesis 2:19-20

The dignity of work is central to our value as human beings. Work can provide a sense of purpose, honor, and hope for the future. When people develop marketable skills and find jobs, they can provide for themselves and their families. They are no longer shamed into begging and reaching for handouts.

Is there a job, ministry role, or hobby you enjoy or that makes you feel alive as you are doing it?

Ruth is new to the community of faith and work, while trusting Yahweh. In Colossians 3:23-24 (NLT), the apostle Paul reminds the people in the church at Colossae: "Work willingly at whatever you do, as though you were working for the Lord rather than for people. Remember that the Lord will give you an inheritance as your reward, and that the Master you are serving is Christ." Paul is setting them straight on who the real master is because slavery and servitude were prevalent in their culture and history; slaves were among the first believers.

Ruth's experience in Boaz's field is a beautiful reminder to all of us that God invites us to work willingly for his glory, not for the purpose of pleasing others. We aren't called to striving or servitude. We are invited to enter into his creative abundance and to honor each other regardless of position.

What is one way you can remind yourself during your daily work that you are serving Christ and not people?

DAY THREE • Danger in the Fields

Dear friend, today's reading and homework come with a trigger warning. We are aware that some of you may have experienced violence or assault in your history. This is an important discussion that rises out of Ruth 2, but you have permission to take a break today and care for your soul if you need to. Check back in with us tomorrow when we talk about God's lovingkindness on display in this chapter.

READ Ruth 2:5-9. What forms of protection did Boaz provide for Ruth?

When Ruth went to glean in the fields, she faced the reality that she could be in real danger as a gleaner. In her book *Finding God in the Margins*, Carolyn Custis James articulates how Ruth risked danger on three different fronts that day when she went out to glean. First, she would have faced other hungry gleaners like herself. A scarcity mentality often prevails when there are limited supplies of food or water. If several gleaners were gathering scraps in the same field, sometimes there would be competition or fights over what was available. Ruth was vulnerable as a young female, a foreigner, and a widow, which would have been obvious by her clothing. She could have been a target for other greedy gleaners.

Second, Ruth faced danger from the hired harvesters in the fields. Although they would have been a notch above the gleaners on the social ladder, they still were lower in the overall power structure. "The tendency among humans to pass their pain and frustrations onto those less powerful and less fortunate is a recurring blight on human history. It happens at every level of patriarchal structures. So for a young, defenseless woman like Ruth, the possibility of sexual assault is present . . . even in the field of Boaz," continues Custis James.

The third level of danger would have been from the landowner himself, who was at the top of the power ladder in these situations. The narrator tells us early on that Boaz is a worthy and honorable man, but Ruth would not have known that information. Before he arrived, Ruth took a chance requesting to move outside the customs and gather more grain than usually was afforded to gleaners. He, too, could have taken advantage of her when he arrived in the field. There are plenty of stories in the Bible and prevalent in our culture today where the person at the top of the social ladder abuses the most vulnerable individual at the bottom.

What we discover in chapter two of Ruth is that Boaz was not that kind of man. In fact, he immediately gave instructions and set boundaries that protected Ruth in his field.

READ Ruth 2:19-23. Why was Naomi glad to hear that Ruth was gleaning in Boaz's field?

In Ruth 2:22 (ESV), Naomi recognized and called out the grace Ruth received in finding Boaz's field.

Unfortunately, I have my own story of facing danger as a foreigner in a different land. When studying abroad in college, I was assaulted by two men on my way to class one day. By God's grace I was spared from rape, but the assault was committed and took its toll on me for years afterward.

After that experience, my best friend and her boyfriend, who were part of my cohort, offered me a protection I am deeply grateful for even to this day. They met me at my house each morning and walked me to class and traveled with me wherever I needed to go. They could not save me from the trauma I had already experienced, but they offered me a sense of safety with their presence. By choosing to go with me, they infused me with courage I did not have on my own. I did not feel alone.

Have you ever had an experience when a friend, sibling, or someone else went with you or offered you protection of some kind? What did that feel like?

Boaz acted as an advocate for Ruth. He stood up for her publicly and protected her in his field. He followed the biblical mandate to advocate for the poor and vulnerable.

Turn back to Proverbs 31. The first part of the chapter, verses 1-9, contains words that were part of an oracle or group of instructions given to King Lemuel by his mother.

Write out Proverbs 31:8-9 in the space below.

Boaz spoke up for Ruth, and in turn Naomi, with his words and actions. Advocacy is amplifying the voices of the marginalized. Throughout the Old and New Testaments, we see God's concern for the vulnerable and his invitation into advocacy. "God loves justice, but also *does* justice," write Matthew Soerens and Jenny Yang in their book, *Welcoming the Stranger*. "From Moses and David to Isaiah and Esther, we see ordinary human beings being used by God to bring his vision of justice to the broken world around them, whether through changes in policy, social structure, or attitudes toward certain groups of people."

Of course, Jesus is our ultimate advocate. He stood in the gap for each one of us and continues to advocate and intercede for us today.

We may be called to advocate for someone else using our passions, convictions, and experiences. Boaz went above and beyond to extend generosity and protection to Ruth. My friends found a simple-but-tangible way to come alongside me when I was vulnerable and helped offer a sense of safety. Let's be in tune to the ways God might be leading us to advocate for the vulnerable around us.

Think of a cause, topic, or group that you feel passionate about. What are some small ways you might be an advocate today? Jot down some ideas in the space below.

DAY FOUR • God's Hesed on Display

As we have learned, one of the most powerful words that describes God's steadfast love for us is the Hebrew word *hesed*. Michael Card in *Inexpressible* explains it this way:

> When we see an act of hesed, an act where someone who has a right to expect nothing is nevertheless given everything, all of a sudden there are tears in our eyes, some sort of inexplicable resonance in our hearts, maybe even the beginnings of a song. Despite the overwhelming evidence all around us that kindness, love, mercy, and grace are a fragile tissue, a delusion, when we see one of those rare evidences of hesed, something, everything within us resonates.

Today let's look at the story of Naomi. Back in Moab, soon after Naomi prayed a blessing of hesed over her daughters-in-law, her attitude changed.

READ her response to the people in Bethlehem in Ruth 1:20-21. What complaints does Naomi levy against God?

Naomi came into Bethlehem with a chip on her shoulder. She was wallowing, depressed, bitter, and frustrated. She felt like she had been forgotten by God—perhaps was even being punished by him. *Don't call me Naomi, which means pleasant, but call me Mara, because I am bitter.*

But God's hesed reappears for Ruth, and for Naomi through Ruth.

How might the provision Ruth received be an example of God's hesed?

How is this a turning point in Naomi's attitude toward Yahweh?

The book of Ruth puts God's hesed on grand display. God's hesed blessed Naomi through the sacrifice and loyal commitment of her daughter-in-law Ruth. God's hesed also benefited Ruth as he showered her with both mercy and abundance through Boaz. And God's hesed raised up the loyal Boaz who grows in generosity and relationships. Hesed is pictured through the coming together of Boaz and Ruth. We are just beginning to see that story unfold in Ruth chapter two.

In Ruth 2, Naomi and Ruth experience a different fullness. How would you describe the fullness they are now experiencing in Bethlehem more than a decade after Naomi initially left?

Naomi is no different from the Israelites who often complained about God's provision. In Numbers 11, there's an example of the people complaining. They were nostalgic about their lives before the wilderness—when they were *slaves* in Egypt.

READ Numbers 11:4-6. What are the Israelites lamenting here? How has self-pity distracted them?

Naomi somehow forgot that the reason she left Bethlehem with Elimelek in the first place was because of a famine. Boaz's generosity toward Ruth in the field wakes Naomi up to the gift of God's hesed. Contrary to what she thought, God was working out plans to care for her and her daughter-in-law in a profoundly personal way.

In his famous play *Les Misérables*, Victor Hugo writes, "The pupil dilates in the night, and at last finds day in it, even as the soul dilates in misfortune, and at last finds God in it." This is a reminder of the same truth David wrote about in the Psalms and Naomi discovered in chapter two of Ruth. Each of these children of God are called out of darkness by God's hesed—that inexpressible mix of divine kindness, extravagant generosity, and persistent faithfulness.

How have you experienced God's hesed in your life?

God gives generously out of his resources. After all, he doesn't just own a barley and wheat field like Boaz. He owns the cattle on a thousand hills (Psalm 50:10). He feeds the birds and clothes the lilies of the field in fancy clothes (Matthew 6:25-34). God through Boaz provides abundantly for these two widows who have experienced hunger and emptiness. How much more does he provide for us!

In Philippians 4:19 (CSB), the apostle Paul deepens our understanding of God's generosity in light of Jesus: "My God will supply all your needs according to his riches in glory in Christ Jesus."

The book of Ruth serves as a testimony to Paul's words. God can and will meet all our needs. In my own experience, he meets those needs in ways we might not ever imagine. God sacrificed his Son, Jesus, as an embodiment of his hesed.

We who live after Jesus' death, resurrection, and ascension can see the continuum of God's constant faithfulness and glorious grace even after Naomi. Iain Duguid in *Esther and Ruth* explains that the father waits for the returning prodigal, with open arms and heart, eager to welcome her home. "He doesn't just allow us grudging admission to glean in his field; he invites us to his table to partake in his feast."

Friend, pray today that God would open your heart to his hesed. You are welcome at the buffet table of his love.

DAY 5 • Reflect

ART AND JOURNALING PRACTICE

The last four days we have been walking through the second part of Ruth chapter two. Today you are invited to take time to slow down, meditate, and reflect. Meditating on Scripture and taking time to respond are important practices.

Give yourself time to look over the chapter and the notes from the last four days. Let the details of the story and the Scriptures we have studied sink in.

Is there a word or truth you learned about this week that was meaningful to you? Write it out below. How does this apply to you in your current season or situation?

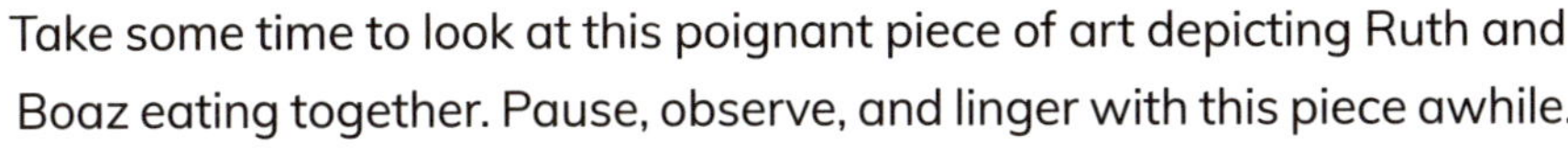

Take some time to look at this poignant piece of art depicting Ruth and Boaz eating together. Pause, observe, and linger with this piece awhile.

What do you see in this artwork?

What about this painting reminds you of what we witnessed this week in Ruth 2:14-23?

What might the Holy Spirit be speaking to you today through this piece of art?

The Bible, particularly the Psalms, help reorient us to what is true about God and his character. **READ** Psalm 118 in *The Message* to help refresh your spirit and remind you of God's attributes and character qualities. Underline or note the qualities that are most meaningful to you.

Is there an area in your life where God could bring healing and spiritual renewal today? Pray and ask the Holy Spirit to bring to mind any areas that need his healing balm. Write about it in the space below or in a journal.

WEEK FOUR

An Unexpected Engagement

RUTH 3

GROUP SESSION: RECLAIMING A LIFE

Each of us is given a choice when we meet the unexpected. We can embrace it or walk away from it. When Shawn got on one knee and asked me to marry him, I had a choice to say yes to a new, unexpected life, or say no and stay stuck in my grief. I realized I could move forward while still honoring my late husband and trusting God for my future.

This chapter of Ruth reminds us that God can reclaim the hardest of circumstances for his glory. Ruth, Naomi, and Boaz have come a long way from where they started. Let's talk about how we are living work-in-progress redemption stories.

WATCH

Take some time now to **WATCH** the video that accompanies the week four study. Then read the Scripture together and discuss the following questions with your group.

READ

READ Ruth 3:1-18.

DISCUSS

1. **Have you ever bought something from a thrift store or antique store or reclaimed a piece of furniture? How did that piece become new when it was washed and put into a new place?**

2. **After watching the video, how would you describe the nuance between the concepts of reclaiming versus redeeming? (You might explore the words' meanings in the dictionary for more clarification of the differences.)**

In the Old Testament context, redemption referred to the release of people, animals, or property from bondage through the payment of a price. In a general sense, redemption was understood as restoration of family property and of well-being.

3. **READ the following Scriptures and share what you notice about where the redemption comes from in these contexts.**

Exodus 6:6

Job 19:25-26

Psalm 31:3-5

4. **God's rescuing Israel from slavery in Egypt was the foundational act of redemption. Can you think of other examples in the Bible where God's redemption power is displayed? Jot them down here and share them with your group.**

5. **READ** Ruth 3:9. Ruth calls Boaz a redeemer in this verse. What does this declaration imply?

Redemption is one of the terms that the New Testament writers use to help us understand salvation. The word *redeem* means to bring new value to something or reclaim as one's own. Redemption is the repurchase of something that has been lost; the payment of a ransom, which is mentioned 129 times in the Bible in its Hebrew form, is required. The Greek word for "redemption" is *apolytrōsis*, a word occurring nine times in Scripture, always with the idea of a ransom or price paid. Redemption is a central theme of the book of Ruth and throughout the Bible. God is in the business of redeeming our lives and reclaiming us as his children.

6. READ the following Scriptures and jot down a few words used to describe what Jesus did to redeem us.

   Matthew 20:26-28

   Romans 3:24-25

   Ephesians 1:7-10

7. How do Boaz and his actions point toward our need for a redeemer?

PRAY

As you close your time, I've included a few suggestions to guide you in prayer together:

- Thank God for the ways he has reclaimed and redeemed your life.
- Ask God to meet you in the current chapter of your life.
- Share any longing you have for reclaiming relationships or situations you face today.
- Ask God to open your eyes to the ways he is making all things new in the community around you.
- If you prefer, you might write out a prayer in the margin or in a journal.

MEMORY VERSE

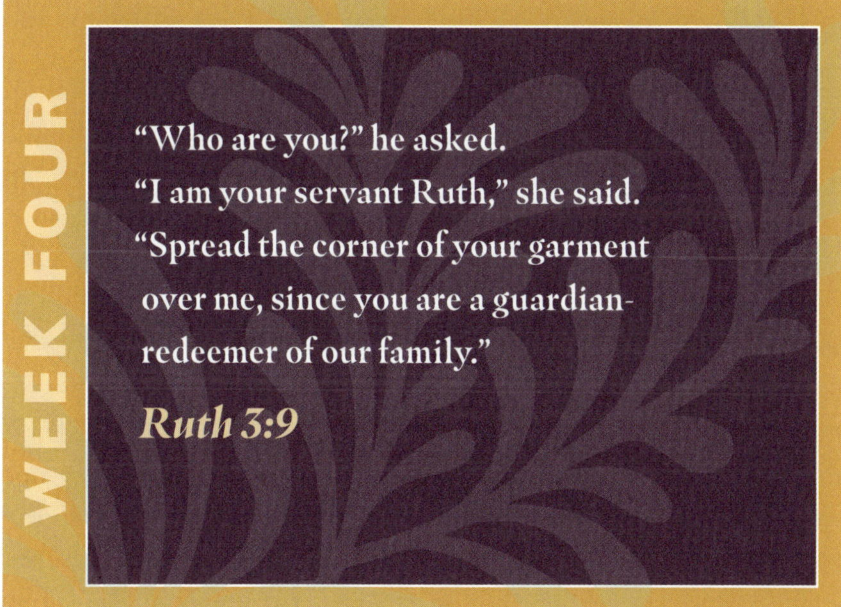

DAY ONE • A Matchmaker on the Job

When it gets close to Christmastime—you know, in October—my daughters and I love to watch Hallmark Christmas movies together. There's something magical about cozying up on the couch with fuzzy blankets and a charcuterie board brimming with snacks. We settle in for a good, predictable chick flick that usually starts with a new love interest, proceeds with a misunderstanding between them, and ends with a kiss. Even though the book of Ruth is a story that focuses on love—with a matchmaker and a surprising plot twist!—it is so much more than a Hallmark romance.

READ Ruth 3:1-18 to familiarize yourself with the developing plot. Jot down any surprises or twists that you notice in the story.

It has likely been several months since Ruth and Boaz met. We know that she has been gleaning in Boaz's field for both the barley and wheat harvests. Cue the music for *Fiddler on the Roof*'s "Matchmaker, Matchmaker" song. We see at the start of this chapter that Naomi has a little matchmaker in her. She says to Ruth, "My daughter, should I not seek *rest* for you, that it may be well with you?" (Ruth 3:1 ESV, italics mine). Interesting choice of words, right?

The Hebrew word *manoakh* is translated here as "rest," but you'll see that other translations use other words to describe what Naomi wants for Ruth.

LOOK UP Ruth 3:1 in at least three other Bible translations. According to these other translations, what was Naomi seeking for her daughter-in-law?

When we discover different translations using different words and terms, we don't need to decide which is best (especially those of us who aren't Hebrew or Greek scholars). Comparing verses in different translations can increase our understanding of a passage, and signal to us the challenges of translation. Words and expressions in different languages often do not share a word-to-word correspondence.

Now look back at Ruth 1:9 and notice the similar language. (We discussed this in week one, day four.) Notice anything? Naomi's love for her daughters-in-law and desire that they would have "rest" let us know that Naomi wanted Orpah and Ruth to experience security, provision, and marriage.

Here in Ruth 3, Naomi unfolds a wild plan for Ruth to approach Boaz with a proposal in search of that rest.

What are Naomi's specific instructions for her daughter-in-law in Ruth 3:1-5?

Some scholars believe this indicates that Ruth had been wearing mourning clothes for many years—far beyond the norm. So perhaps Naomi is asking Ruth to trade her mourning clothes for a party dress. But it's more likely that she is concerned for Ruth's safety and is instructing her to remain a bit incognito. Kathleen B. Nielson in *Ruth and Esther* explains that the threshing floor was an open-air structure where the sheaves of grain were winnowed, a process of separating the grain from the chaff. The harvesters often stayed at the threshing floor after a long day of work to eat and drink and guard the grain.

However, Naomi's plan wasn't foolproof. Why? We talked about the culture clash between the Moabites and Israelites in week one, day three. God had warned them against intermarrying with people who did not follow Yahweh. (The story in Numbers 25 offers further context for why the Israelites stayed away from Moabite women.)

Based on this history, what are the risks for Ruth?

Ruth was choosing to stay hidden, as Naomi advised, because her very presence might have been viewed as a moral threat. She was a Moabite, and a woman on the threshing floor might also have been viewed as an invitation to sexual promiscuity. Many men have justified abuse and sexual sin when women were alone in outdoor, isolated places at night. Because we know Ruth's character, we know there's no trace of shadiness or sexual duplicity in her motives.

In a traditional matchmaking situation, the father would have negotiated the marriage arrangement and a girl's mother would be present.

A dowry would often be offered, which was a payment made by the bride's family to the groom. In other cases, a bride price would be offered, which was a payment of money or goods made by the groom to the bride's family. And both—either a dowry paid to a groom or a bride price paid by the groom—were determined by the perceived value of the bride. Regardless, when a marriage was arranged, it involved a commitment of the bride and groom as well as of both families.

LIST all the factors that keep Ruth from following protocol for an arranged marriage.

Remember that Ruth has been instructed by Naomi to wait until after the dinner party is over and to observe where Boaz lies down to sleep. Then after Boaz is satisfied and sleeping, Ruth is to go in, uncover his feet, lie down, and wait for him to tell her what to do. This is the plan. But Ruth goes a bit off-script.

READ Ruth 3:6-9. What is Ruth's request to Boaz in Ruth 3:9?

This is the moment of tension that every good movie plot contains. We don't know what will happen next. We don't know how Boaz will respond to this unexpected marriage proposal of sorts.

Ruth is there on the threshing floor, fending for herself, while Naomi is back home praying. This is a moment of courage and truth for the young believer, Ruth.

Ruth is a woman of integrity and resolve. Even though she is walking into an uncertain future, her character remains intact. In day two we will discuss more about the risk Ruth was taking with her proposal, but today let's center on the courage of this woman to call out her redeemer.

Lord God, thank you for Ruth's example of faithfulness and boldness to ask Boaz to protect her and to step in as her family's guardian-redeemer. Help me to walk in spirit and truth, confident in your care, as Ruth did. Amen.

DAY TWO • Taking a Risk

In Ruth 3, we witness Ruth courageously stepping forward to carry out the plan Naomi laid out for her. Ruth used her agency and added her own twist. She prepared, waited, and laid at Boaz's uncovered feet. Typically, this would have been a place near a sleeping man that was reserved for a wife. This gesture communicated that she was interested in becoming his wife through the custom of *redemption*.

As we discussed in this week's group session, redemption is a theme in Ruth, but it's also a central theme throughout Scripture. God is in the business of redeeming our lives and reclaiming us as his children.

Boaz was startled awake when he felt someone at his now uncovered feet. "Who are you?" he asks (Ruth 3:9). Can you imagine? An older guy of integrity with a Moabite widow a few decades younger sleeping at his feet? Put yourself in Boaz's sandals for a minute.

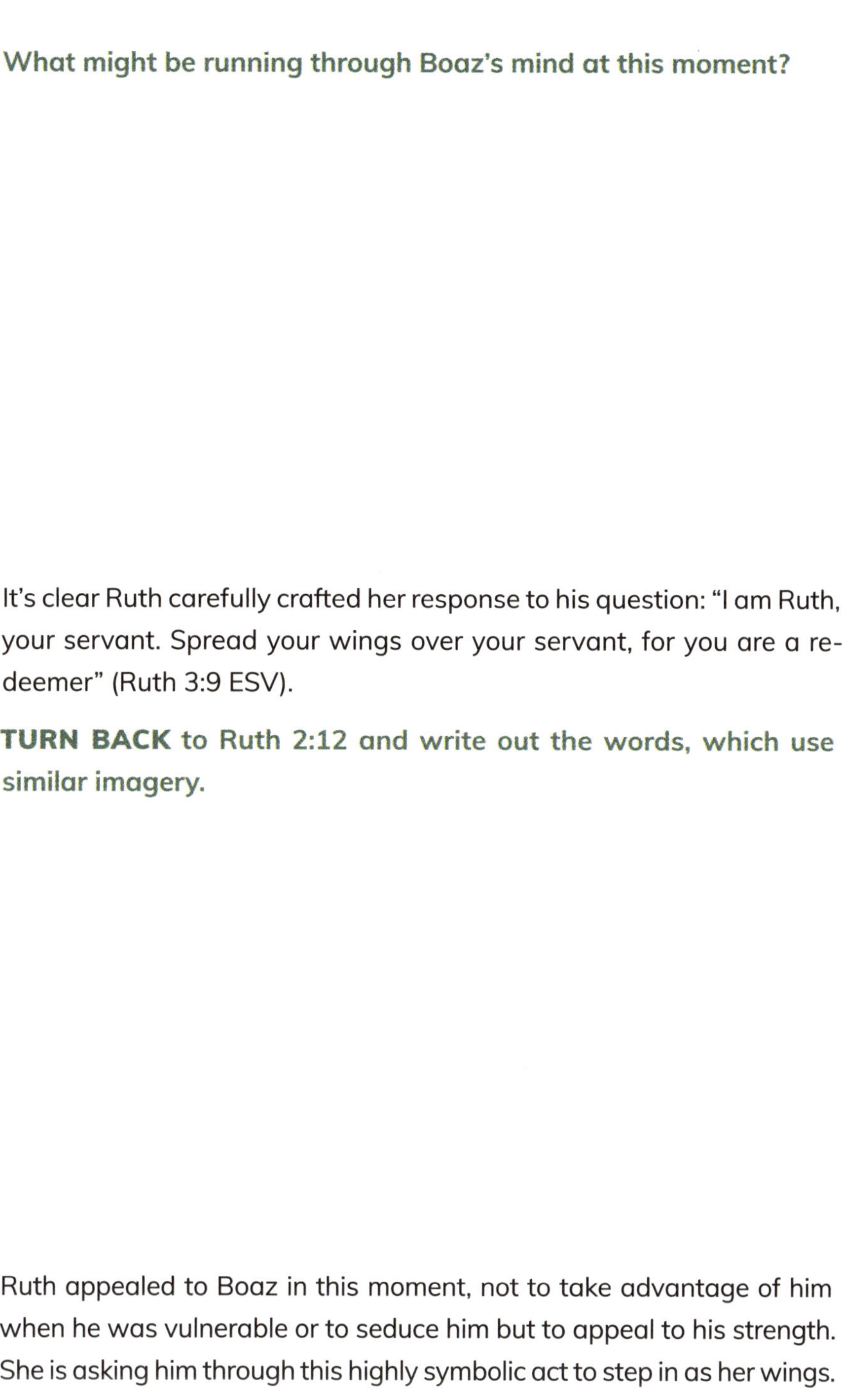

What might be running through Boaz's mind at this moment?

It's clear Ruth carefully crafted her response to his question: "I am Ruth, your servant. Spread your wings over your servant, for you are a redeemer" (Ruth 3:9 ESV).

TURN BACK to Ruth 2:12 and write out the words, which use similar imagery.

Ruth appealed to Boaz in this moment, not to take advantage of him when he was vulnerable or to seduce him but to appeal to his strength. She is asking him through this highly symbolic act to step in as her wings.

LOOK UP the following verses that also use wing imagery. What do wings represent and how do these verses help you understand what Ruth was requesting?

Psalm 17:7-9

Psalm 57:1

Isaiah 40:31

The other day I saw a photograph of a mother bird with wings extended like arms around her two bird babies on either side. At a quick glance, the babies looked like they were an extension of the mama's body because they were enveloped by her feathers. The mama bird protectively wrapped her wings around her chicks in the same way God wraps his arms around us. When we are hidden in his shadow or under his wings, we are protected like a baby bird from the elements and from the enemy who hunts us down. We are not left vulnerable and out in the open but protected in a safe place. The Bible does not promise us there will be no trials or heartache in this life, but it does assure us that Immanuel will be with us.

"Garment" and "wings" are two words often used interchangeably in Hebrew. Let's look at Ruth 3:9 in a different translation to help us understand further the implications here. "'Who are you?' he asked. 'I am your servant Ruth,' she said. 'Spread the corner of your garment over me, since you are a guardian-redeemer of our family'" (Ruth 3:9). The New International Version emphasizes the word *garment*, rather than *wings*. Part of Naomi's instructions were that Ruth uncover Boaz's feet and lie there. He would have likely covered his feet with his garment or skirt. Ruth was now asking Boaz to cover her with his garment.

Today in many parts of the East, if a man says he put his skirt over a woman or covered her, it is synonymous with saying he married her. At modern marriages of Jews or Hindus, one part of the ceremony is for the bridegroom to put a silken or cotton cloak around his bride to symbolize this covering.

What Ruth did and said was risky. She presented herself to him for marriage. This young widow was declaring her eligibility—not to everyone but specifically to Boaz. And that makes Ruth vulnerable. What we know about Ruth is she has moxie. But also, God is on her side. Thankfully, Boaz did not have cold feet when it came to Ruth's proposal. He responded with grace and honor.

READ Ruth 3:10-13. What do you notice about Boaz's response to Ruth?

Boaz understood that Ruth's proposal was more than a romantic proposition. In fact, there's no hint in the Scriptures that love or romance was involved. Elimelek and Boaz were close relatives, and Ruth was asking him to redeem her, which meant protecting Elimelek's land as well as marrying her and caring for Naomi. She is asking for a combination of the levirate marriage law and the guardian-redeemer law that were part of Jewish customs.

Let's go back to learn more about the law concerning levirate marriage that Ruth is referring to here.

READ **Deuteronomy 25:5-10. What do you understand about the expectations under the levirate law?**

Meanwhile, there's the guardian-redeemer law described in Leviticus 25:25, which we will look at more in depth on day four. This law focused on the land and included a wider range of relatives beyond just the brother-in-law. According to this law, the nearest relative (or guardian-redeemer) was called to step in and purchase the land or reclaim it from the outsider in order to keep his relative's property in the family or tribe. Both laws required immense sacrifice.

We all face puzzling predicaments in life and find ourselves at a crossroads like Boaz. We must choose our own self-interest (comfort, security, well-being, and the like) or choose to sacrifice for others.

Have you ever been at a place where you had to choose between sacrifice and self-interest? What was that like for you?

Jesus is our Guardian-Redeemer. He is our covering and provides rest.

Friend, you can experience his rest today under the covering of his wings.

Jesus, shelter my heart and provide the strength I need as I look to your help to navigate through the difficult circumstances I am facing today. Amen.

DAY THREE • Saying Yes to Trust

We can trust God even if we don't know or understand all the details of our situation. Ruth took a risk. She trusted Yahweh first. She trusted Naomi's plan. And ultimately, she trusted Boaz and his character when she stepped forward and asked him to redeem her. He could have taken advantage of her, but he didn't.

LOOK UP Proverbs 3:5-6 in the translation of your choice. Write out the words in the space below. What do these verses teach you about God?

One of the hardest parts for me of stepping into a new relationship was trusting again. My heart was broken when my husband died. My heart felt like it was a shattered glass that couldn't ever be repaired. It was hard to hold on to hope and imagine a redeemed future.

Maybe some of you can relate. Maybe you have been betrayed or you are navigating a broken relationship. Maybe you are widowed, divorced, or single and feeling uncertain about the future. Maybe you've walked through some kind of loss, abuse, or trauma. When your heart has been shattered, it's hard to step out in trust and hold on to hope.

I struggled to believe God could redeem my story. I worried that pursuing a relationship with Shawn would mean more heartbreak for my girls and me. At the core of it, I was afraid to risk loving someone again.

One morning I was up before the sun, sitting in our front room on our big red couch reading my Bible. We had a beautiful Japanese maple tree in our front yard. I loved watching how her leaves would change colors through the seasons and dance in the breeze. On that particular morning, I was journaling my prayers. I cried out to God to give me peace and clarity about dating Shawn. I remember looking up and seeing my late husband Ericlee sitting next to me on the couch. He told me gently, "It's okay. This is what I would have chosen. I know Shawn will care for you and the girls. I trust him."

Just as quickly as he appeared, he was gone. God used that vision to steady my heart and give me confidence to step forward in a relationship with Shawn. We might not always have a vision in tough situations and uncertainty, but the Lord faithfully provides guidance in many ways.

Think of a decision or situation that made you feel uncertain. What was most helpful as you sought clarity and wisdom?

In Ruth 3:10, Boaz started by blessing her and calling her daughter. Remember in the past Ruth has often been referred to as a Moabite or as a woman. She has been held at arm's length, stereotyped, and put into a category by everyone except Naomi. Boaz speaks to her with tenderness and familiarity, calling her "daughter" just as Naomi does. Some commentaries say this indicates the age difference between Boaz and Ruth. The text doesn't give us all the details, but we know that daughter is a term of endearment.

Read Mark 5:25-34. In Mark 5:34, Jesus uses this same term of endearment to address a woman who suffered from bleeding for twelve years. "He said to her, 'Daughter, your faith has healed you. Go in peace and be freed from your suffering.'"

This woman was an adult, but Jesus intentionally calls her "daughter"—the same word that Boaz uses for Ruth.

Why might Jesus have used this term? How would this have been meaningful to her?

The old adage says, "Sticks and stones may break my bones, but words will never hurt me." This couldn't be further from the truth. Words have the power to pierce our hearts or empower us. The woman who reached out to touch Jesus' garment feared humiliation and shame. She didn't push to meet Jesus or talk to him because she didn't want to draw attention. She believed he could heal her and reached out. *And she is the only person in the New Testament to be called "daughter" by Jesus.* This word daughter honors and empowers the woman who bled for twelve years just as it honored Ruth.

LOOK UP Ruth 3:10. How does Boaz acknowledge Ruth's sacrifice?

The word *kindness* is translated as "family loyalty" (NLT) or "loyalty" (NRSV and a few other translations). This is the third appearance of that beautiful Hebrew word *hesed* in the book of Ruth. (Flip back to week one, day four and week three, day four to remind yourself of what you've already learned about hesed.)

What does Boaz's use of hesed here indicate to us about his character and his intentions regarding Ruth?

The Message version of Ruth 3:10 invites us into the emotion of the moment: "He said, 'God bless you, my dear daughter! What a splendid expression of love! And when you could have had your pick of any of the young men around. And now, my dear daughter, don't you worry about a thing; I'll do all you could want or ask. Everybody in town knows what a courageous woman you are—a real prize!'" Boaz doesn't just reluctantly agree to this assignment. Ruth didn't work hard to persuade him. He eagerly stood up as the redeemer. In Ruth 3:11 Boaz encouraged Ruth by saying, "Do not fear" (ESV) or "Don't you worry about a thing" (MSG).

READ Ruth 3:11. How does Boaz honor Ruth and her character in this verse?

That's right. Boaz reminded Ruth that she is an *eshet khayil*, that same Hebrew word used in Proverbs 31:31 we studied on week one, day two. His words were filled with kindness and promise. We can imagine that these are rungs on the ladder of trust for Ruth.

God, thank you that you continue to work behind the scenes, gently guiding me toward redemption and trust in you. Ruth and Boaz lived this out in courageous ways; oh, give me some of what they had and lead me to trust in your providence. Amen.

DAY FOUR • Stepping into the Shoes of a Guardian-Redeemer

Boaz chose to display *hesed* when he stepped into the redemption story. He was not the nearest relative, nor was he Elimelek's blood brother. Ruth invited Boaz to be her redeemer (*goel* in Hebrew), who is charged with the duty of restoring the rights of another and avenging wrongs against them.

READ Ruth 3:12-13 and Leviticus 25:25, 47-54. From these passages, what do you understand about the law of the guardian-redeemer?

These verses unfold the details of how the guardian-redeemer law worked. They also clarify that Boaz was under no obligation here. When we realize Boaz is not the next-of-kin, there's a little cliffhanger in the story. This would be the moment when a TV network would take us to a commercial break or a writer would pause to let us wonder before starting a new chapter. We wait with bated breath.

READ Ruth 3:14-18. What passes between Ruth and Boaz in the morning?

This gesture underscores his kindness and generosity. Sending Ruth home with the gift of grain may also have been a nod at the Jewish custom of the bride price. We see an example of this in Genesis 29 when Jacob offered to work for seven years for Rachel's father, Laban, in exchange for her hand in marriage. These negotiations are still used in some countries, such as India, Bangladesh, Pakistan, Sri Lanka, and Nepal.

Boaz hands over a generous gift—likely more than sixty pounds of grain, which would have been quite heavy for Ruth but also expresses the weight of his commitment!

And if this is indeed a bride price from Boaz to Naomi (Ruth's family)—a custom that was based on the perceived value of the bride for the groom—what does Boaz's gift indicate?

Boaz exemplified the kind of generosity that Paul writes about in one of his letters to Timothy. Paul was correcting the false teachers and their view of wealth, urging the people to care more about eternal riches than earthly riches (1 Timothy 6:17-19).

Boaz was a rich man. He used his resources to help care for the vulnerable—in this case Ruth and Naomi. His example is a beautiful model to us of how we can multiply the riches God has given us. Boaz was not a perfect man, but he bravely stepped into the shoes of a redeemer. He went beyond the letter of the law—for both guardian-redeemers and levirate marriage—and embraced the true spirit of these laws.

What are some ways you could implement this principle in your daily life?

As we've seen, the theme of redemption is prevalent throughout Scripture. So when we hear that Jesus "did not come to be served, but to serve, and to give his life as a ransom for many" (Matthew 20:28), we shouldn't be surprised!

He came to earth in a human body so he could be a close relative to us on earth. He was willing to do his father's will and redeem us. He was also able to pay the ransom price. That his body and his life are the ransom offered tells us that redemption comes at a high cost. Jesus came to rescue the exploited, to restore the brokenhearted, to revive the weary, to reclaim the marginalized, and to redeem all who believe.

Jesus is our ultimate Guardian-Redeemer.

If you have had an experience with redemption in your life or witnessed it in another's life, what was that like?

Friend, I want to challenge you today to think about the places where God is calling you to be generous. We can be generous with our resources, our time, our talents, and our presence. Let's not just be rule followers. Let's follow God's model that goes above and beyond. He was generous with us in sending his one and only Son as our redeemer.

WRITE down one small way you can share your resources, time, talents, or presence to bless someone else. Include who, what, and when in your plan.

DAY FIVE • Reflect

ART AND JOURNALING PRACTICE

The last four days we have been walking through all the action and drama of Ruth 3. Today you are invited to take time to slow down, meditate, and reflect. Give yourself time to look over the chapter and the notes from the last four days. Let the details of the story and the Scriptures we have studied sink in. Take some time to reflect on what you learned this week about taking risks, building trust, and redemption.

What is one takeaway you want to hold on to?

Take some time to look at this poignant piece of art. Pause, observe, and linger with this piece awhile. What do you see in this artwork?

What about this painting reminds you of what we witnessed this week in Ruth 3?

What might the Holy Spirit be speaking to you today through this piece of art?

Now read through Psalm 19. Psalm 19 offers us reminders of how creation and the law (or God's Word) lead us back to his character and redemption. Pay attention to any specific words or phrases that help you understand God and his character better.

Are there images or scenes this psalm brings to mind for you? Take some time to journal here about how this psalm meets you today.

WEEK FIVE

Redemption in a Wedding

RUTH 4:1-13

GROUP SESSION: BEARING WITNESS IN COMMUNITY

Getting married when I was twenty-five and then thirteen years later at age thirty-eight with three daughters in tow were two vastly different experiences. God was in the process of bringing beauty from ashes. The death of my husband Ericlee was not the end of us—although it felt like that on some days. It was the closing of a chapter with many new chapters to be written and lived out. Let's talk in our groups today about how we have witnessed the power of redemption in our own lives and communities.

WATCH

Take some time now to **WATCH** the video that accompanies the week five study. Then read the Scripture together and discuss the following questions with your group.

READ

READ Ruth 4:1-13.

DISCUSS

1. **Can you think of a moment when God made something new in your life or when he brought good from a bad situation? Maybe it was a wedding, the day of your baptism, an anniversary, or another event. Share a bit about this day of remembrance for you.**

In today's video, I talked about the "cloud of witnesses" who were present with us for our wedding day. The phrase "cloud of witnesses" here looks back to Hebrews 11, where God's faithful people from the past are named and acclaimed. They are like boisterous fans in a stadium cheering us on.

2. **Take three minutes to scan Hebrews 11. What stands out to you about the cloud of witnesses?**

3. **READ Hebrews 12:1-2. Think about the power of community in your life. Who are the members of the cloud of witnesses for you?**

4. When Naomi and Ruth arrived in Bethlehem, they seemed isolated, and we sometimes are too. What factors led to their isolation? If you feel on the fringes of things, what factors contribute to that?

5. The importance of community is a theme throughout Scripture. READ the following passages. What does each reveal about biblical community?

   Acts 2:42-47

Colossians 3:12-15

Hebrews 10:24-25

6. READ Ruth 4:9-11. Boaz redeemed the land and Ruth in the presence of witnesses. Why do you think it was important for Boaz to do this in community?

7. When Boaz spoke with the guardian-redeemer at the city gate, the guardian-redeemer is initially enthusiastic. But he declines to redeem the property. Why?

8. It has been said that Boaz (Ruth's guardian-redeemer) and Jesus (our Guardian-Redeemer) are similar in character and action. What are some common qualities that you noticed?

PRAY

In today's video, I shared how Shawn was an integral part of our community and rose up in obedience to God to partner with our family. Discuss and then pray with your group about any creative ways God would have you rise up in this season to care for or reach out to someone in your community. Are there ways you can bear witness to the work God is doing in a friend or family member to encourage them?

If you prefer, write out a prayer in the margin or in a journal.

MEMORY VERSE

WEEK FIVE

He gives strength to the weary
and increases the power of the weak.
Even youths grow tired and weary,
and young men stumble and fall;
but those who hope in the LORD
will renew their strength.
They will soar on wings like eagles;
they will run and not grow weary,
they will walk and not be faint.

Isaiah 40:29-31

DAY ONE • With Us in the Waiting

Last week we concluded our study of Ruth chapter three with these poignant instructions from Naomi: "Wait, my daughter, until you find out what happens. For the man will not rest until the matter is settled today" (Ruth 3:18).

Ruth and Naomi are both left waiting. There's a pregnant pause in the action of the story. They are wondering and wishing, perhaps doubting and dreaming, about what is to come. This situation could go several directions, but Naomi's words hold a confidence because she knows Boaz's track record, and she's trusting Yahweh.

READ Ruth 4:1.

This verse tells us Boaz went up to sit at the city gate. This was a significant place in each city. Read the following Scriptures, which give us glimpses into the importance of the city gate in its cultural context.

Referring to the verses below, what kinds of things typically happened at the city gates? How would you characterize the importance of this place?

2 Samuel 15:1-4

Job 29:4-12

Proverbs 31:23

The city gate often served as a combined city hall and courthouse. This was the place where elders often witnessed transactions and decided on legal cases. It was the center of the action. Boaz goes there to settle the guardian-redeemer matter. And it *just so happens* the redeemer who is a closer relation to Naomi than Boaz passes by. We will read more about that in detail tomorrow.

But in the meantime, Naomi and Ruth remain on standby. At that time, women were not included in gatherings at the city gate. So even though they trust Boaz, they are dependent on him to take the next steps. And so they wait.

Waiting is part of our everyday lives, but it is not wasted time. Ann Voskamp writes in her book *Waymaker*, "Nothing is lost in the waiting process because all waiting is a growth process. Waiting is gestating a great grace. Maybe life has no waiting rooms—life only has labor and delivery rooms. All our waiting rooms are actually birthing rooms, and what feels like the contraction of our plans can be the birthing of greater purposes."

When my late husband was battling cancer, we spent a lot of time in waiting rooms to see doctors, waiting to get treatments, and waiting to hear the next prognosis. The waiting often felt long and excruciating. Maybe you've sat in the waiting room too. Maybe you've been waiting for that diagnosis or for a prodigal child to come home. Maybe you've been waiting for reconciliation in that relationship. Maybe you've been waiting for some solution to your financial stresses. In the waiting we may find ourselves longing for more information or crying out to God for guidance. Waiting can be hard and character shaping.

Recall a season in your life when you were waiting for a long time. What were you waiting for and what did you do in the meantime?

Looking back, was there any benefit to the season of waiting?

Growth and purpose can rise from our seasons of waiting. This resonates with the words of the prophet in Isaiah 40. The prophet Isaiah warned Israel that God was the only one who could protect them from Babylon and Assyria, the military powers of the day. The people did not trust Isaiah's prophecy. Instead they relied on their own strength, strategy, and even threw in some sacrifices to false gods for good measure. Israel had to pay the consequences for their disobedience. Yet Isaiah 40 presents a hopeful look to the future when the people are trusting God again.

READ Isaiah 40:28-31. What happens while we wait for the Lord, according to these verses?

Different translations and versions of the Bible use different words in place of that English word "wait." Looking at these helps us get a fuller picture of what the prophet Isaiah was saying. We are called to "hope in the LORD" (NIV), to "trust" in him (HCSB), and to "wait upon" him (MSG) for our next move. When we trust and wait for God, he leads us in surprising ways to fly like eagles.

Eagles are fascinating, majestic birds that have long, large wings. Their bodies are light with bones that are hollow. Their skeletons weigh only about one-half pound, but their wings are very strong. When eagles fly, they flap their wings only a few times to gain altitude. Then they spread those wings and use wind thermals to help them soar through the air, which conserves energy.

Wind thermals are big gusts of wind that rise above the atmosphere. Eagles perch for long periods of time (sometimes days), waiting for that just-right wind thermal that will take them the furthest. Like the eagles, we also must wait with anticipation and hope. God is with us in the waiting. He can direct us when it is time to flap our wings and catch that wind thermal. While we are waiting, God can infuse us with that renewed strength and resolve.

As we close today, let's settle in to this thought. The Israelites waited hundreds of years for the coming of the Messiah. They waited through dark nights and uncertain times. They waited when the future looked bleak, the enemy drew near, and loved ones died. They waited and watched through four hundred years of silence between the last prophet Malachi's words and Matthew's Gospel that gives us the good news of the ultimate Guardian-Redeemer born in Bethlehem. Friend, there is purpose in our waiting.

Let's pray quietly for a minute as we breathe, repeating:

(INHALE) *Jesus, my Guardian-Redeemer,*

(EXHALE) *I wait for you.*

DAY 2 • Redemption Is a Process

The story line of Scripture from Genesis to Revelation is the story of God's redemption. The word *redemption* or *redeemed* is used twenty-three times in the entire book of Ruth. The words *redeem* and *redeemer* are repeated several times throughout this chapter of Ruth.

READ Ruth 4:1-7. Underline or highlight the word *redeem* or *redeemer* in this passage. Taking what you have learned about redemption thus far, why is this significant?

Redemption by a guardian-redeemer (*goel*) was the most common form of redemption in the Old Testament. This guardian-redeemer was a close male relative from the same clan.

As we read about in Leviticus 25:25 in week four, day four, the closer the familial relation, the greater the obligation to redeem on behalf of the family member in need. The spirit of this law was that anyone who could redeem a relative should, but the greater responsibility was to the nearest relative.

Let's take some time to dig into the details of the process Boaz goes through to redeem the land and ultimately Ruth and Naomi. Look back at Ruth 4:3-4.

What do you notice about the way Boaz characterized the situation to the other redeemer? Is there any strategy you detect in his words?

The unnamed redeemer heard about the land and immediately says, "I will redeem it" (Ruth 4:4). We can almost hear the eagerness in his voice. Then Boaz explains that the day the man buys the land, he will also inherit Ruth.

READ Ruth 4:5, 10. How does Boaz refer to Ruth? Why is this significant?

This is the turning point as the unnamed redeemer is considering the situation. It's not just about multiplying his land anymore. If this man chooses to step in as the guardian-redeemer of the land, he would jeopardize his own inheritance. Although this man is not Elimelek's brother, Boaz suggested that the man marry Ruth and have children to carry on Elimelek's name and keep the land in the family. The kicker is that if they had a son together, that young man would be Elimelek's heir of record and would eventually inherit the land, not the redeemer's first-born son. (The same applied to Boaz, but since it isn't mentioned, it doesn't seem to concern him.)

REREAD Ruth 4:6. Why does the "redeemer" (the closer relative) pass on Ruth?

We can almost imagine him raising his hands as if to say, "I don't want anything to do with this."

Of course, this is exactly what Boaz wanted. Boaz was considered an upstanding man with clout in the community. No one stepped forward to oppose his plan, which clearly comes from a generous heart. He continued the process of redeeming the land and Ruth in the presence of the witnesses. This shows us Boaz's attention to proceeding with integrity and in accountability within the community.

READ Ruth 4:9-12. What is the response of the people and the elders who were at the gate?

It's significant to notice that three women from Israel's history are referenced in this blessing. Rachel and Leah were the wives of Jacob, later named Israel, and mothers (with maidservants Zilpah and Bilhah) of the men the tribes of Israel were named after.

This phrase about Rachel and Leah was also culturally significant because it was the usual bridal benediction. This blessing may have been delivered at Boaz and Ruth's wedding or at a public ceremony.

It might not be as clear as to why the people mentioned Tamar here.

Tamar was a childless widow, like Ruth. According to Jewish law, she should have become the wife of Judah's son Shelah, but Judah sent her home. Tamar's only righteous option was to use deceit to became pregnant by Judah. Despite her tragic history, Tamar's life was redeemed as she became the mother of Judah's strongest son, Perez, who was an honorable man and fathered many children who continued the line of Judah. Tamar was a foreigner, marginalized, overlooked, and ostracized. Like Ruth, she married an Israelite man and was widowed. She exhibited courage, kindness, and a deep loyalty to the family.

Genesis 49 includes Jacob's blessing of his sons, including Judah: "The scepter will not depart from Judah, nor the ruler's staff from between his feet, until he to whom it belongs shall come and the obedience of the nations shall be his" (Genesis 49:10). This is an arrow pointing to Jesus, the Redeemer, who will come through the line of Judah and Perez.

It's a pretty big deal that they are comparing Ruth the Moabite to these three women! This shows their high esteem for Ruth. "We are witnesses. May the Lord make the woman who is coming into your home like Rachel and Leah, who together built up the family of Israel" (Ruth 4:11).

God is invested in the process of redemption. He is there from start to finish. He reclaimed Ruth and Naomi—and Boaz too—just as he reclaims me and you. And the community rejoices to see it. Pray this prayer with me:

Dear Lord,

Thank you for this wonderful story showing your character as my Guardian-Redeemer.

Help me to always remember how the lives of Leah, Rachel, and Tamar illustrate how much value you place on me, especially during difficult times.

Amen.

DAY 3 • Welcoming the Outsider

The marriage of Ruth and Boaz is a coming together of two people from different cultures and different sides of the tracks. Through Ruth and Boaz, our Author God is continuing to write the grand redemption story. He is bringing together Jews and Gentiles, which the apostle Paul called the great "mystery" of the gospel. It may not seem like such a huge mystery to us, sitting where we are in history today—after Jesus was born, ministered on earth, died on a cross, rose again, and was raised into glory. But it was a profound mystery then.

Paul opened the book of Romans with a long greeting that proclaimed the mystery of the gospel to Roman readers he did not know and underscored God's heart for the nations.

READ Romans 1:1-6 and take note of Paul's use of the phrase "all the Gentiles" (verse 5). Some translations say "all the nations." Why is this significant?

Paul's opening highlighted his own mission to the Gentiles, the non-Jewish peoples, or "the nations." He wanted Roman readers to know from the beginning of this letter that they are all included in the gospel of Jesus Christ. They are invited to the table.

Of course, this was a radical invitation when Jesus made it and when Paul reiterated it later. Jewish believers were not rolling out the welcome mat to non-Jewish believers, as God did in the Old Testament for people like Hagar and Ruth. Jesus came and modeled what it looked like to welcome outsiders to dine at God's table and be part of his kingdom. This is the true redemption—that *all* who believe are welcome!

How do you respond personally to this mystery? What does it mean to you that Gentiles (or non-Jews) are included in this invitation?

READ Galatians 3:26-29, which is Paul's encouragement to the church in Galatia. How does he echo this same idea here?

As Paul boldly writes, we see evidence all throughout the Scriptures that God's *hesed* love is for all the people of all the nations. Psalm 117 (ESV) is a short, two-verse psalm that underscores this point and calls all people to praise the LORD, Yahweh:

> Praise the Lord, all nations!
>
> Extol him, all peoples!
>
> For great is his steadfast love toward us,
>
> and the faithfulness of the Lord endures forever.
>
> Praise the Lord!

Again we see that emphasis on "all nations." That phrase "steadfast love" is his hesed toward all people, which "endures forever."

LOOK UP the following examples from the Old Testament:

Genesis 17:5; 1 Kings 8:59-60; Isaiah 56:6-7

What do you learn about God's heart through these verses?

God's plan to redeem his people from all nations extends throughout the story line of the Bible. Here are a few of the highlights that point toward that ultimate redemption talked about in Revelation:

- God saved Israel from slavery in Egypt (Exodus 6:6).
- God redeemed Israel from Babylonian exile (Jeremiah 16:14-15).
- God called his people holy and the "Redeemed of the Lord" (Isaiah 62:12).

- God sent his Son, Jesus, to live, die, and be raised again (John 3:16).
- Jesus ascended to heaven, where he will dwell with his father until the Grand Wedding (Acts 1:6-11).

Boaz and Ruth continue to point to God's hesed and his heart for the vulnerable and specifically for the outsider. This couple represents more than an unexpected connection. Together they are a picture of biblical justice, which is God's heart for the vulnerable and mending the brokenness in our world.

Dr. Martin Luther King Jr. in his speech "Where Do We Go from Here?" said, "Power at its best is love implementing the demands of justice, and justice at its best is love correcting everything that stands against love." Boaz leveraged his position and power to redeem Ruth. Consider the unnamed redeemer and how he was really in it for personal gain, while Boaz was more interested in caring for Ruth, the outsider, at his own personal cost. Boaz used his power and acted out of love.

Similarly, Ruth sacrificed her life in Moab and followed Naomi to Bethlehem. She worked to care for Naomi and used her own agency to pursue marrying Boaz, which was both gutsy and strategic. Ruth and Boaz together display the character of God: Both sacrificed for each other. Both embody love, mercy, and grace, which is the heart of God's hesed.

Consider your own life. How has someone sacrificed for you?

In *The Invitation*, Eugene Peterson tells us, "Ruth is the inconsequential outsider whose life turns out to be essential for telling the complete story of God's ways among us." Peterson reminds us that God is intentional to use all kinds of people to further the story of redemption. Ruth was an outsider who was brought to the inside and given a place of honor in the kingdom and the story line of the Bible. The same is true for each one of us. Through Jesus, we are invited to step inside the circle of God's hesed.

Close your eyes and imagine the circle of God's hesed for Naomi, Ruth, and Boaz. Then, in your mind's eye, approach and step into the circle, thanking God for his faithfulness and lovingkindness.

DAY FOUR • A Heavenly Wedding

The narrator of Ruth made it sound like this story was "first comes love, then comes marriage, then comes a baby in a baby carriage." I suspect there's so much more between that first sentence of Ruth 4:13 and the second sentence of that same verse. In fact, it's quite possible there were years between them. We can't help but wonder: *What would an established Jewish man marrying a converted Moabite woman have been like?* What we do know is that Boaz and Ruth coming together in Bethlehem in this moment in history would have been out of the ordinary.

READ the first part of Ruth 4:13. What do you imagine Ruth and Boaz's wedding might have been like?

I have to admit, I'm a little sad we don't have more detail in the text about their wedding. I may be biased, but multicultural weddings are my favorite because they are such a sweet opportunity to celebrate God bringing people together from diverse places, cultures, and customs.

When my husband Ericlee and I got married, we promenaded down the aisle following a bagpiper to honor Ericlee's Scottish heritage. At the reception, I removed my shoes and danced the traditional Hawaiian wedding dance to honor my Polynesian ancestry and my grandparents' home. This is a generations-old tradition in my dad's family. My mom danced it for him at their wedding, and my grandma danced it at her wedding. We had Italian pizzelle cookies that my Italian mama made for dessert to add to the multicultural buffet.

As I shared in the video this week, Shawn and my wedding was a celebration of God's glory and the community of friends and family who had supported my daughters and me through our grief journey. My daughters and a host of friends were involved in the ceremony at our church, which was followed by a dessert reception put together by my church's moms' group.

Later that evening, we dined and danced at a hall downtown called The Grand. It was indeed grand! There were so many kids in attendance that they took over the dance floor, with my three daughters at the center of the action. Friends drove in from the Bay Area and Los Angeles, and some flew in from the East Coast, which Shawn had called home for more than nine years.

Our wedding—similar to Ruth and Boaz's wedding—was an unexpected union. God was highlighting the miracle of his grace in our lives. He brought together a grieving widow and a worthy man both motivated by God's *hesed* and woven together by the thread of providence.

Wedding imagery and descriptions of weddings are highlighted throughout the Bible. We have several examples that show weddings as a key place of community gathering, celebration, and blessing in Jewish culture. In the Old Testament, we read about the wedding feast arranged by Laban (Rachel and Leah's father) described in

Genesis 29. In a New Testament wedding, Jesus turned water into wine at his mother Mary's prompting and commenced his public ministry (John 2).

Jewish weddings included many traditions designed to point to the covenant of marriage and God's partnership with his people. In Hebrew, a wedding is called a *simkhah* (a joyous occasion). Traditionally, the bridegroom would wear the *kittel*, which is a white linen garment symbolizing purity, holiness, and new beginnings. The bride would wait in her home in her wedding garments until the groom came for her. The wedding was symbolic of a couple's commitment to their marriage.

READ Isaiah 62:5. How does this verse point to God's ultimate redemption?

Revelation 19 is a picture of a wedding that represents the ultimate justice and flourishing God has for us in the future. The church is depicted as the bride of Christ who will meet her bridegroom face to face.

READ Revelation 19:6-9. What do you learn about this wedding to come?

These verses you just read are a call to worship and rejoicing. We will be able to "re-joy-ce" or return to joy when we (the church) are reunited with the Lamb (Jesus Christ). In many ways, Ruth and Boaz's wedding points to the wedding of the Lamb described in Revelation.

Let's read the vision of the new heaven and earth that John shares in Revelation 21:1-14. How does he describe the bride, and what does this imply?

I love how this passage reminds us in verse 5 that God, who is sitting on the throne, is making *everything* new. This brings us back to the redemption story that is the heart of the book of Ruth and unfolds through biblical history into the book of Revelation. Because of God's hesed, we will one day be united in marriage with Jesus Christ. We will have the opportunity not just to attend but to be part of a heavenly wedding that far exceeds any ceremony or celebration we have experienced here on earth. That is something to look forward to!

Let's celebrate with John as he ends his description of this wedding: "Amen. Come, Lord Jesus" (Revelation 22:20).

DAY FIVE • Reflect

ART AND JOURNALING PRACTICE

The last four days we have been walking through all the nuance and wonder of the first part of Ruth 4. Today you are invited to take time to slow down, meditate, and reflect. Give yourself time to look over the chapter and the notes from the last four days. Let the details of the story and the Scriptures we have studied sink in. Take some time to reflect on what you learned this week about taking risks, building trust, and redemption.

What is one takeaway you want to hold on to?

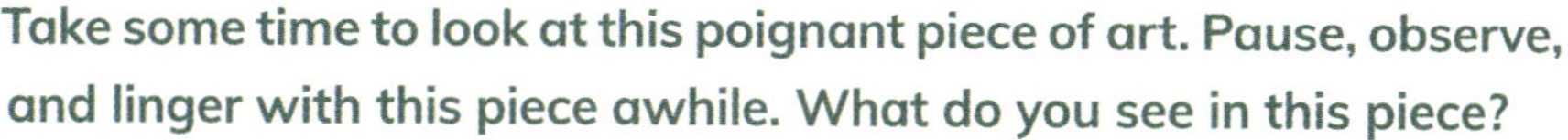

Take some time to look at this poignant piece of art. Pause, observe, and linger with this piece awhile. What do you see in this piece?

What about this painting reminds you of what we witnessed this week in Ruth 4?

What might the Holy Spirit be speaking to you today through this piece of art?

Psalm 30 illuminates how God brings joy from our seasons of grief. READ Psalm 30 in the New Living Translation. Underline or note any words or phrases that teach you about God's character and how he meets us in trials and grief.

How does this chapter grow your appreciation for the *hesed* love of our Redeemer?

What is the Holy Spirit bringing to mind as you reflect today? Are there any action steps you might pursue as a result of this time?

WEEK SIX

A New Branch in the Family Tree

RUTH 4:14-22

GROUP SESSION: GRAFTED INTO GOD'S FAMILY

The book of Ruth invites us to consider the concept of adoption and being grafted into God's family. In many ways, Ruth (and you and me) being grafted into God's family tree is a reversal. Let's discover why.

WATCH

Take some time now to **WATCH** the video that accompanies the week six study. Then read the Scripture together and discuss the following questions with your group.

READ

READ Ruth 4:14-22 aloud.

DISCUSS

1. **In today's video, I talked about how Shawn chose to adopt my daughters eight years after we were married. However, God had given him a heart for adoption years earlier through his own family story. What passion, skill, or experience did God give you years ago that you are using or pursuing today? How might God use that?**

2. Think about a time when you experienced a reversal in your life—something that changed the course of your life and moved you in the opposite direction. Share the story with your discussion group.

3. What have you learned these last five weeks about God's heart for the vulnerable?

4. READ Galatians 4:4-5. The New International Version notes that "adoption to sonship" refers "to the full legal standing of an adopted male heir in Roman culture." What do you learn from these verses about God's plan for our adoption into his family?

5. Adoption in our Christian faith often refers to the receiving of a believer into God's family. Now read Romans 8:14-17. What is the role of the Holy Spirit in our adoption?

6. Let's return to the book of Ruth together. READ Ruth 4:14-15. These were the words spoken to Naomi by her friends and community. Why do you think these words were significant to hear at the close of the story?

7. How do you feel about being invited and welcomed into God's family?

PRAY

As you close your time, I've included a few suggestions to guide you in prayer together:

- Ask God to show you what it looks like to be a son or daughter adopted into his family.
- Pray against any thoughts that make you feel "less than" or unwanted.
- Thank God for the invitation to be adopted into his family.
- Pray for eyes to see others and welcome them into God's family.
- If you prefer, write out a prayer in the margin or in a journal.

MEMORY VERSE

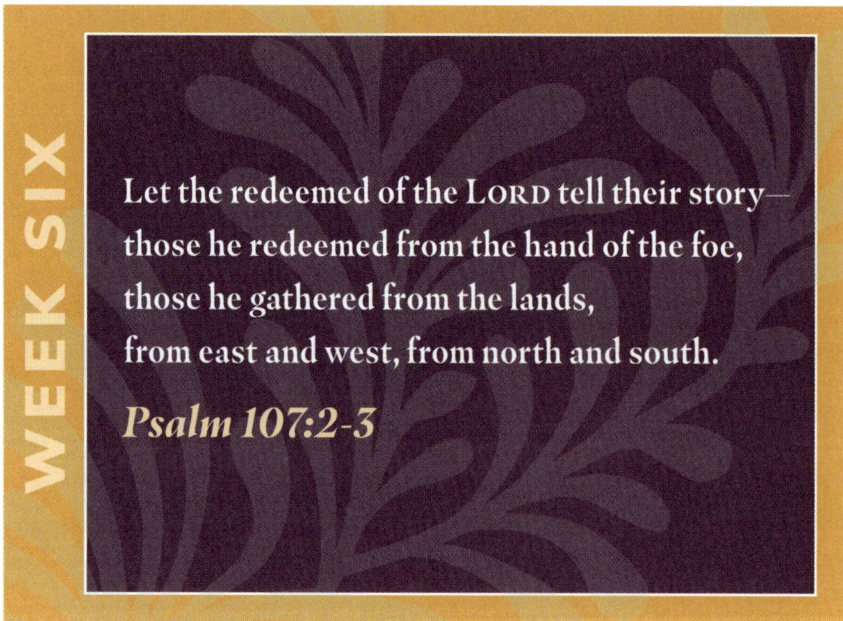

DAY ONE • Witnessing Regeneration

There's a fiery, red-orange freesia that blooms every spring outside my front door. I did not plant her there. She was an unexpected gift that came with our house when we bought it. Her beginning is a bulb that burrows deep in the hard earth of winter and then breaks through to produce new life year after year. She is a fragrant flower—her scent a kind of herald, announcing a new season, a resurrection.

Like the freesia, we must weather our own winters before we can experience the warming colors of spring. We must face seasons of brokenness, grief, and death before we can taste the victory of resurrection. We must endure Good Friday to arrive at Easter Sunday.

There is a process that happens in the heart during a winter of grief. Tears can water the soil of our hearts. I found that rather than abandoning me, God was with me in my grief. He wept with me. He comforted me in the dark places. These words from John 16:33 became real to me there: "I have told you all this so that you may have peace in me. Here on earth you will have many trials and sorrows. But take heart, because I have overcome the world" (NLT).

Jesus reminded me through these verses that we will all face trials and suffering, but we can have hope in him. He chose to die a literal death on a cross so that we might experience an eternal life in heaven. The story of Ruth illuminates this tension between death and life, between grief and hope, between fear and courage. God gives us permission to grieve and invites us to move forward toward his glory.

In the last five weeks we have witnessed God's heart for the vulnerable. He sees Ruth and Naomi as his daughters and provides for them in surprising and miraculous ways. Chapter four may be seen as the culmination of the book of Ruth. This chapter illuminates the lavishness of God's *hesed* for his children.

Ruth experienced the regenerative work of God in her life after she chose to follow Yahweh to Bethlehem. Regeneration is the transformation of a person's spiritual condition from death to life through the work of the Holy Spirit. The word regeneration literally means a "new birth." The Greek word *palingenesia* is used by classical writers to refer to the changes produced by the return of spring. It's like that flower pushing through bulb stage to bloom.

Ruth chose to leave Moab where she was spiritually dead and where she had buried her husband. She journeyed to Bethlehem, which means the "house of bread" and represented provision. As we venture into this final section of the book of Ruth, let's reflect on the transformation that happens in Ruth and all the main characters.

READ Ruth 4:14-22. What would you put on a highlight reel of this section of Scripture?

If we were to assign seasons to the book of Ruth, chapter four feels like spring. This season includes a wedding, a baby, and new branches added to God's family tree.

We left off last week thinking about Boaz and Ruth's wedding celebrated in Ruth 4:13. The latter part of that verse is already talking about the conception of a baby. Needless to say, there's a lot going on in that one verse!

READ the following translations of Ruth 4:13.

> So Boaz took Ruth, and she became his wife. And he went in to her, and the LORD gave her conception, and she bore a son. (ESV)
>
> Boaz married Ruth. She became his wife. Boaz slept with her. By GOD's gracious gift she conceived and had a son. (MSG)
>
> So Boaz took Ruth and she became his wife. When he made love to her, the LORD enabled her to conceive, and she gave birth to a son. (NIV)

What are the nuances or differences you note?

Ruth and Boaz could be considered a match made in heaven because they both possessed godly character and came together in hesed love. Their relationship was built on the foundation of godly character—not physical attraction and romance, which we elevate in Western culture.

After the wedding, Boaz and Ruth are united physically, and God allowed the childless Ruth to bear a baby. Remember there is no mention of any children conceived or born in the ten years Naomi was in Moab and her sons were married (see Ruth 1). This is further evidence of regeneration in Ruth's life and Naomi's too.

Why is it significant that God is the one who enables Ruth and Boaz to conceive?

This is only the second time God is mentioned as acting in the book of Ruth. There is no mistaking that his providence is working throughout the book and allows this child to be conceived for his purposes. God brings glory out of Ruth's grief.

Ruth joined the ranks of several other courageous women of the Bible who had their barrenness reversed at God's hand, but after years—even decades—of waiting. Let's take some time to recall a few of those stories and how the babies became adults God used for kingdom purposes.

READ the following passages and jot down the names of the mothers and sons mentioned in them.

Genesis 21:1-3

Genesis 25:21-26

Genesis 29:32-35

1 Samuel 1:19-20

Ruth is counted among these miraculous mamas. Each of these women endured an immense amount of grief in their histories. None of them was perfect or pedigreed, and their problems didn't disappear in an instant, but God chose to open their wombs and use them to mother children who were added to his family tree.

Whether you are a mother or not, how do you relate to these women? Can you identify with their pain or grief or long period of waiting? Write out a prayer to God about your thoughts in the space below.

Friend, our God might not redeem your story in the way he redeemed it for Ruth and Boaz. The reality is that not every barren woman later births a rainbow baby. Not every widow gets remarried to a Boaz. Not every single or divorced woman finds that worthy man. But that doesn't mean God isn't at work and bringing redemption to our lives in unique ways. In fact, the transformation in Ruth is not about finding the perfect man or birthing the baby at all. It's about regeneration of her faith and moving toward God's perfect Son, her Redeemer for eternity. Keep your eyes open for the unexpected ways God might be ushering you into unexpected comfort and a reversal of your heaviest grief.

DAY TWO • Full Arms

In Ruth chapter four, we see Naomi back on the scene—this time in full celebration mode with the women from her community and a baby in her lap.

READ Ruth 4:14-17. Who are "the women" mentioned in verses 14 and 17 and why is it significant that they are present in this scene?

These women help name the blessings in Naomi's life. There are three significant character qualities of God they call out. Circle them in the verses below.

> Then the women said to Naomi, "Blessed be the Lord, who has not left you this day without a redeemer, and may his name be renowned in Israel! He shall be to you a restorer of life and a nourisher of your old age, for your daughter-in-law who loves you, who is more to you than seven sons, has given birth to him." (Ruth 4:14-15 ESV)

Think back over the last five weeks of study. REREAD Ruth 1:20-21. How has God been these things for Naomi? How has she changed from the beginning of the book to the end?

The women bless Yahweh and praise his provision of a redeemer, restorer, and nourisher in Naomi's life. When Shawn and I got married, an added blessing extended to his mother, Florence. At the time, Florence had been struggling through years of chronic illness. When the girls and I met her, she was very frail and stayed mostly at home in bed. She did make the journey to our wedding, which was a three-hour drive from her home in Southern California.

She celebrated because her son, who had been single for forty years, was marrying. Florence was also gaining three new granddaughters. Now she has five granddaughters and one grandson between our family and Shawn's sister's family. That was doubling her grandkid count all at once!

My mother-in-law was widowed more than two decades ago. Her husband (Shawn's father) died of a stroke in his sixties. Although the context of Florence's story is very different from Naomi's story, we have also witnessed a miraculous reversal in her life. Her health has significantly improved over these last eight years. She loves to engage with her grandkids—writing them cards, playing games with them, attending events, and spoiling them as grandmas love to do.

Naomi, too, gained a renewed sense of purpose by the close of the book. She is not a discarded, destitute woman. She is not a wayward widow. She is a gregarious grandmother to baby Obed. Her arms were empty when she arrived in Bethlehem at the end of chapter one, but now they are full at the close of chapter four. She is living back home in Bethlehem and helping to raise her grandson.

Perhaps you have also felt like your time had expired or your purpose was out of date. Maybe you had a dream that hasn't come true after years of waiting. Maybe you've endured profound loss and you're having difficulty imagining how God can bring a reversal to your circumstances.

Each of our stories is unique, but how might principles from Naomi's story encourage you?

This child is a miracle, not just because of the reversal of Ruth's barrenness but also because he is the fruit of God's reclaiming Naomi. The Scripture says, "Naomi has a son!" (Ruth 4:17). Even though Obed is Ruth and Boaz's son, he is like a son to Naomi. Remember, according to the customs of that time, Obed would be known as part of Elimelek's lineage—not Boaz's! And because Obed has been grafted into Elimelek and Naomi's lineage, she contributes to the care for him. Her future is also secure because this grandson will care for Naomi as he grows and she ages. He will continue her family's legacy.

The women of the community also name Ruth as "better to you than seven sons" (Ruth 4:15). This is a high honor because sons were often valued more than daughters in this culture. And yet, this gives us an example of a daughter-in-law who is elevated because of her sacrifice and loyal love for her mother-in-law.

Seven is a number used throughout the Bible as a symbol of perfection. This is a beautiful and deserving tribute the "cloud of witnesses" give to Ruth.

Describe a woman who has been a blessing in your life (like Ruth) or a mentor (like Naomi). Share about her here and consider contacting her today to thank her for her influence on your life.

At the close of chapter four, Boaz also has full arms. Ruth challenged Boaz to embrace the spirit of the gleaning and redeemer laws, to go beyond leftovers. He goes above and beyond to offer these women lavish love and provision. Both Ruth and Naomi are redeemed because of Boaz's generosity and willingness to heed Ruth's advice. Boaz is stronger because of his encounter with Ruth and Naomi. There is synergy in their coming together.

The book of Ruth is so often cast as a love story with Boaz as the romantic lead and hero, but after our careful reading we have seen that this is actually a story about what Carolyn Custis James in *The Gospel of Ruth* calls "the Blessed Alliance"—two image bearers, male and female, joining forces to advance God's kingdom together.

Custis James writes, "In the end, there is deep respect, mutual submission, and a powerful partnership that rocks the community, multiplies *hesed*, and secures the royal line of Christ."

This book is about how God uses men and women together to carry out his plans and exemplify true flourishing. Let's not miss that in our Western longing for romance and tying up story lines with neat bows. This is not happily ever after for Ruth and Boaz. Their purpose is bigger than a wedding and a baby. Their arms are full because they point to another history-making child who will be born in Bethlehem in the years to come.

"For to us a child is born, to us a son is given, and the government will be on his shoulders. And he will be called Wonderful Counselor, Mighty God, Everlasting Father, Prince of Peace" (Isaiah 9:6). These words from the prophet Isaiah remind us again that Jesus is the hero of this story and all the stories in the Bible.

Remember this book takes place in the dark time of judges—a long season of violence, betrayal, sexual misconduct, and God's people turning away. The book of Ruth offers a counterpoint of abounding hope and hesed love. Friend, let's take some time today to sit and contemplate the beauty and the bigness of this story.

DAY THREE • The Purpose of Family Trees

As we read through the Bible, we discover that God's family tree had its share of twisted branches and unexpected stories as well. His family tree brings together people of diverse nations and backgrounds. We might be tempted to skip over those lists of names and genealogies in the Bible, but they are significant.

READ Ruth 4:18-22. Using this genealogy, think about the family tree with Naomi and Elimelek at the top alongside Salmon and Rahab, Boaz's parents. What do you notice about the names? Why is it significant that this genealogy ends with the name David?

The genealogy in chapter four reminds us that Boaz and Ruth's son is Obed, who became the father of Jesse, who was Daddy to King David himself. Genealogies were especially important to Israel, and they kept meticulous records. Genealogies emphasized the importance of family and legacy in Jewish culture. The Jews were serious about their responsibility to continue the line that would bring honor to the family name.

Many of these records that we find in Ruth 4 are also detailed in 1 Chronicles.

COMPARE Ruth 4:18-22 to 1 Chronicles 2:5-15, which includes a genealogy featuring Boaz, Obed, and Jesse. Do you notice anything different in that account?

In Ruth 1:16, we read Ruth's pledge to her widowed mother-in-law Naomi that changed everything: "Your people shall be my people, and your God my God" (ESV). She took a leap of faith and pledged to join Yahweh's family with her heart. Ruth was willing to become a heart family member.

What are the implications of Ruth the Moabitess being invited into God's family tree?

Ruth was great-times-forty-grandma to God's own Son, Jesus, our ultimate Redeemer relative. Like Ruth, we are invited into God's family tree when we choose to believe in Jesus, his death, and his resurrection.

My mama's great-grandparents immigrated to the United States from a little town called San Giovanni en Fiore in Southern Italy. Their three sons represent the three main branches of our family tree from which the various generations originated. More than three decades ago, my mama started researching our family tree. Some form of the family tree is always displayed when we gather for our family reunions every few years. Behind every name and every branch is a story. These stories weave together our past and present.

Through the years, we have also welcomed unexpected branches and stories into our family tree—a cousin who married a Japanese American woman, several who have spouses with Latin roots, and my mama who married my mixed-race dad, who is Filipino, Chinese, and Polynesian. Now it's more the norm to find names among the branches that are different from the Tonys, Marias, Franks, Angelas, and Giuseppes, which were more common in the first generation. It's the beautiful mixing of cultures and settling in new cities that make our family tree unique today.

Truth be told, sometimes family trees can be messy. The branches become gnarly and tangled. Some branches are broken off way too soon because of divorce, separation, or death. We might be tempted to hide these stories, but they are an important part of God's redemption story too. In my case, my husband Ericlee died of cancer at age forty. We could view that as a broken branch of our family tree, but God brought my new husband, Shawn, and grafted him in.

What is the story that your lineage tells? Are there any redemption stories you know about that are represented in your family tree?

Even our own family trees can point us back to our place in God's family. We have to stay close to our Daddy God and root ourselves in our identity as his kids. In Paul's letter to the church at Colossae, he talks about the importance of staying rooted: "And now, just as you accepted Christ Jesus as your Lord, you must continue to follow him. Let your roots grow down into him, and let your lives be built on him. Then your faith will grow strong in the truth you were taught, and you will overflow with thankfulness" (Colossians 2:6-8 NLT).

In the Colossian church there was a problem with dangerous, false teachings creeping in. Paul provides both warnings and teachings through his letter encouraging the people to find their identity in Christ and follow him alone.

Friend, remember you are chosen for God's family. You are not an accidental or peripheral branch. You were invited in on purpose. Your story may just be unfolding like a new shoot on the family tree. When we stay rooted in this truth, building our lives on our relationship with Jesus, then our faith will be strengthened.

Let's make Colossians 2:6-8 (NLT) personal and pray it back to God:

And now, just as I have accepted Christ Jesus as my Lord, help me continue to follow him. Let my roots grow down into him, and let my life be built on him. Then my faith will grow strong in the truth I was taught, and I will overflow with thankfulness. Lord, let it be so. Amen.

DAY FOUR • Jesus' Family Tree Is All About Adoption

The concept of adoption is central to the gospel and the redemption story of the Bible. God doesn't just have concern or pity for the marginalized. He welcomes them into his family.

As we have studied the stories of people such as Hagar, Rahab, and Ruth, who were not Israelites but were adopted into God's family, we have witnessed the depth of God's love for the vulnerable. In week five, day three, we delved into the book of Romans and God's heart for the outsider. Paul was writing to the Romans, who were Gentiles. He longed for them to understand this theme of adoption as well.

READ Romans 8:15-17 and Romans 8:23-24. What do you learn about adoption and how is it connected to the gospel message?

Why is it meaningful to you that God uses the language of adoption when he talks about bringing you into his family?

We most likely are Gentiles. We are immigrants, refugees, and marginalized people. And we are adopted into his family. This is part of God's redemption plan for his people. We are invited as his own sons and daughters no matter our background, our culture, or our family of origin.

This is the mystery of the gospel unpacked in the New Testament. God was not interested in a family tree that was only Jewish. He wanted people from Samaria and the ends of the earth in his family.

We are not guilty or excused by association with family members who have faith. We are each granted the freedom of choice to believe in Jesus as our Savior. Then we are given full rights as daughters and sons of the Guardian-Redeemer, the King. Ruth was welcomed into this family—not by default but by God's design.

Matthew, the former tax collector who became a disciple of Jesus, is the author of the book of Matthew. He begins the book with a genealogy of Jesus—a map of his family tree. Matthew aimed to show that Jesus is the ultimate fulfillment of God's promise to Abraham in Genesis 12.

READ the genealogy in Matthew 1:1-17, which includes Rahab, Boaz, Ruth, and Obed. What do you notice that is different in this genealogy compared to Ruth 4:18-22 and 1 Chronicles 2:5-15, which we read yesterday?

If we look at the New Testament, Matthew's Gospel, written for a Jewish audience, traces Jesus' genealogy to Abraham. Luke's Gospel, written for Gentiles, traces Jesus' genealogy all the way back to Adam (Luke 3). This was meaningful for their respective audiences because it showed how Jesus' roots reached through the soil of history. Matthew may have drawn from 1 Chronicles for some of the details included in this genealogy. He omitted several of the kings mentioned in Judges—perhaps for the purpose of tracing the history more quickly.

If we dig into Boaz's family line a bit further, we see that he is the direct descendant of Nashon, the tribal chief of Judah. In Genesis 49:9, Jacob blessed his son, Judah, and called him a "lion's cub." The lion was a symbol of power, royalty, and majesty, and some believe that Jesus is later called the Lion of Judah because he descended from this tribe through Boaz and Obed's line.

READ Revelation 5:5 below. Notice the words *root* and *lion*.

> Then one of the elders said to me, "Do not weep! See, the Lion of the tribe of Judah, the Root of David, has triumphed. He is able to open the scroll and its seven seals."

Given what we have learned this week, why do you think these metaphors or symbols were used to describe Jesus, the Messiah? How do they point to his purpose?

Just as with every book of the Bible, Jesus is the grand finale of the story. Ruth, Naomi, and Boaz have pointed like arrows to his coming throughout all four chapters of their story. God reclaimed their lives, and he continues to reclaim yours and mine.

The book of Ruth has taught us that we serve a God of abundance, not scarcity. He plans to prosper us as his adopted kids, and not to harm us. He is our Guardian-Redeemer, who is always defending us, reaching for us, loving us, and working on our behalf.

Let's conclude our time today by praying a blessing written by Paul to the church at Ephesus that reminds us who we are in Christ. Consider reading it out loud.

> All praise to God, the Father of our Lord Jesus Christ, who has blessed us with every spiritual blessing in the heavenly realms because we are united with Christ. Even before he made the world, God loved us and chose us in Christ to be holy and without fault in his eyes. God decided in advance to adopt us into his own family by

> bringing us to himself through Jesus Christ. This is what he wanted to do, and it gave him great pleasure. So we praise God for the glorious grace he has poured out on us who belong to his dear Son. He is so rich in kindness and grace that he purchased our freedom with the blood of his Son and forgave our sins. He has showered his kindness on us, along with all wisdom and understanding.
>
> God has now revealed to us his mysterious will regarding Christ—which is to fulfill his own good plan. And this is the plan: At the right time he will bring everything together under the authority of Christ—everything in heaven and on earth. (Ephesians 1:3-10 NLT)
>
> Amen.

DAY FIVE • Reflect

ART AND JOURNALING PRACTICE

Over the last six weeks, we have walked through the book of Ruth together. Today you are invited to take time to slow down, meditate, and reflect one final time. Give yourself time to look over the chapter and the notes from the last four days. Let the details of the entire story of Ruth take root in your heart. Take time to reflect on what you learned this week about family trees and adoption.

What is one takeaway you want to hold on to?

Take some time to look at this poignant piece of art. Pause, observe, and linger with this piece awhile.

As Psalm 107:2 says, "Let the redeemed of the LORD tell their story." We have a call to tell the story of God's redeeming love in our lives. The book of Ruth helps us to see it more clearly. Friend, as you and I conclude this journey through Ruth, let's remember the depth of God's *hesed*. Let's look for ways we can "see and rejoice" in this steadfast love, and tell others about it.

MORE RESOURCES

FOR MORE BIBLE STUDY RESOURCES and to access the "Redeemer" music playlist, hop over to www.DorinaGilmore.com and sign up for her weekly Glorygram and freebie library. You can also download a template for Scripture memory cards complementing each section of the study.

Notes

WEEK TWO: THE MEETING

43 *Jewish men are the ones*: Rachel Held Evans, "3 Things You Might Not Know About Proverbs 31." *Rachel Held Evans* (blog), May 12, 2014, https://rachelheldevans.com/blog/3-things-you-might-not-know-about-proverbs-31.

46 *Boaz a warrior and wealthy*: Philippe R. Stirling, "Boaz and Ruth—A Royal Lord and Lady," Vista Ridge Bible Fellowship, March 2, 2015, http://www.vistaridgebiblefellowship.com/blog/boaz-and-ruth-a-royal-lord-and-lady.

WEEK FOUR: AN UNEXPECTED ENGAGEMENT

98 *laid at Boaz's uncovered feet*: John Currid, "Ruth," TGC, accessed March 5, 2024, www.thegospelcoalition.org/commentary/ruth/.

101 *Today in many parts of the East*: R. Jamieson, A. R. Fausset, and D. Brown, *Commentary Critical and Explanatory on the Whole Bible*, vol.1 (Oak Harbor, WA: Logos Research Systems, 1997), 174-75.

WEEK FIVE: REDEMPTION IN A WEDDING

124 *city gate often served*: *ESV Women's Study Bible*, Ruth 4:1-2 (Wheaton, IL: Crossway, 2020), 402.

127 *Like the eagles*: Dorina Lazo Gilmore-Young, *Walk Run Soar: A 52-week Running Devotional* (Bloomington, MN: Bethany House, 2020), 12.

128 *the closer the familial relation*: P. Lau, "Redemption" in J. D. Barry, et al., eds., *The Lexham Bible Dictionary* (Bellingham, WA: Lexham Press, 2016).

131 *phrase about Rachel and Leah*: R. Jamieson, A. R. Fausset, and D. Brown, *Commentary Critical and Explanatory on the Whole Bible*, vol. 1 (Oak Harbor, WA: Logos Research Systems, 1997), 175.

139 *Jewish weddings*: "Ancient Jewish Wedding Customs and Yeshua's Second Coming," The Messianic Prophecy Bible Project, accessed March 5, 2024, https://free.messianicbible.com/feature/ancient-jewish-wedding-customs-and-yeshuas-second-coming.

WEEK SIX: A NEW BRANCH IN THE FAMILY TREE

152 *regeneration literally means*: M. G. Easton, *Illustrated Bible Dictionary and Treasury of Biblical History, Biography, Geography, Doctrine, and Literature* (New York: Harper & Brothers, 1893), s.v. "Regeneration."

159 *Seven is a number*: Tony Merida, *Ruth For You* (Charlotte, NC: The Good Book Company, 2020), 125.

166 *Lion of Judah*: J. Bermender, "Lion of the Tribe of Judah" in J. D. Barry, et al., eds., *The Lexham Bible Dictionary* (Bellingham, WA: Lexham Press, 2016).